Part 01:
01 Descriptions

Part 01:
01 Actions

Part 01:
01 Characters

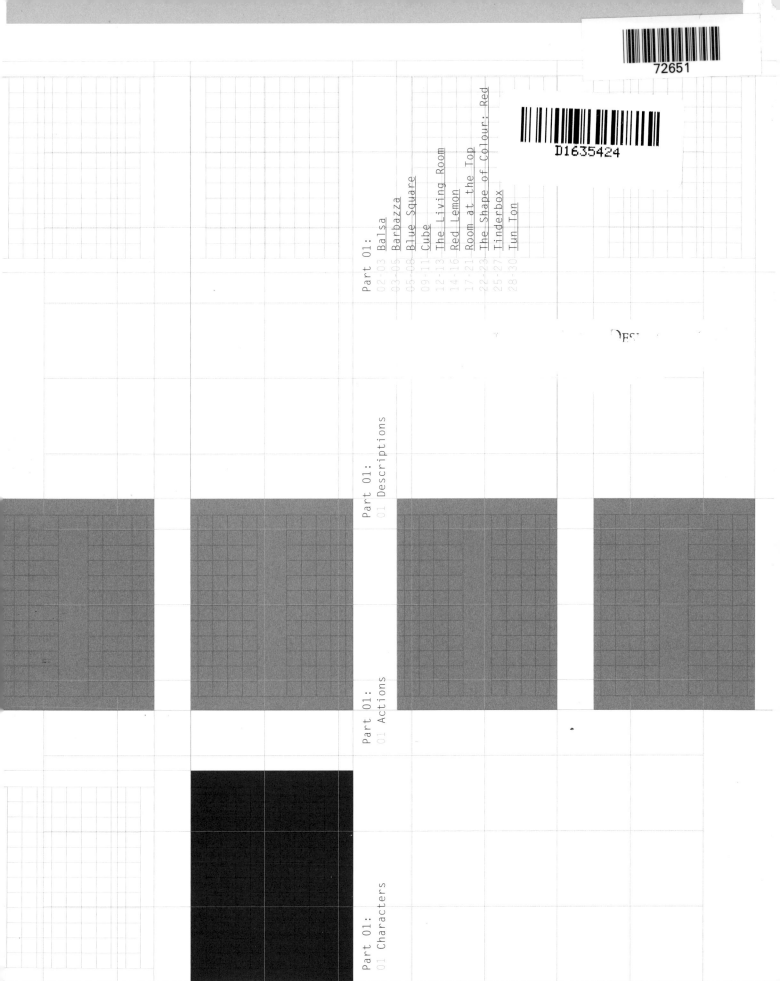

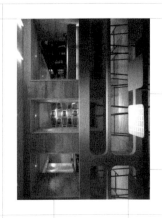

Balsa 01

Balsa 02

Balsa 03

Balsa 04 A

Part 01:
02 Balsa

The idea of crossover is a key element in the approach Graven Images take to design. In some cases, such as Balsa, a bar interior in the centre of Glasgow, a particular leitmotif binds the whole together. Here the designers played with a variation on the letter 'B' - flattened, made symmetrical and with rounded corners - applied in different guises for the entrance canopy, screening and the repetitive wall-decoration pattern. Rectangular forms with curved corners, a knowing reference to early 1970s clubland chic, have become a staple, almost clichéd, element in contemporary-style bar design. But when Graven Images used them for this project back in 1999, the idea was still shiny and new. Graven Images set out to capture a whole new generation of young people with groovy 1970s design cues, accepting the role of bars in the fashion-conscious lifestyle of young Glasgow as much as in the more obvious signifiers of clothes and music. Who you are - or perhaps who you wish to be - is partly defined by where you socialise; quasi-tribal identity has long been part of Glasgow's

Part 01:
02 Descriptions

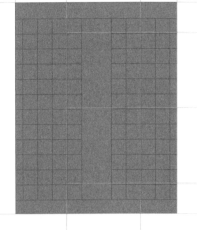

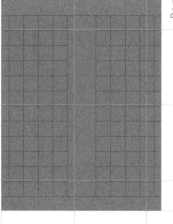

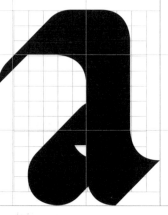

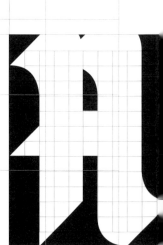

Part 01:
02 Characters

Character a

Character A

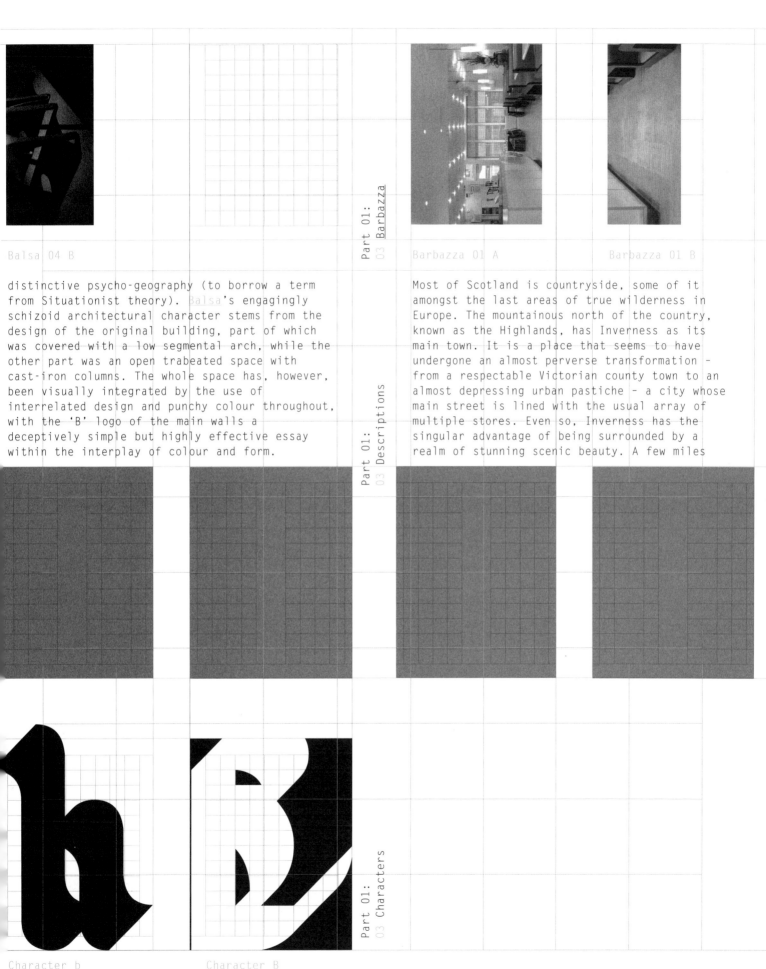

Balsa 04 B

Barbazza 01 A

Barbazza 01 B

distinctive psycho-geography (to borrow a term from Situationist theory). Balsa's engagingly schizoid architectural character stems from the design of the original building, part of which was covered with a low segmental arch, while the other part was an open trabeated space with cast-iron columns. The whole space has, however, been visually integrated by the use of interrelated design and punchy colour throughout, with the 'B' logo of the main walls a deceptively simple but highly effective essay within the interplay of colour and form.

Most of Scotland is countryside, some of it amongst the last areas of true wilderness in Europe. The mountainous north of the country, known as the Highlands, has Inverness as its main town. It is a place that seems to have undergone an almost perverse transformation - from a respectable Victorian county town to an almost depressing urban pastiche - a city whose main street is lined with the usual array of multiple stores. Even so, Inverness has the singular advantage of being surrounded by a realm of stunning scenic beauty. A few miles

Character b

Character B

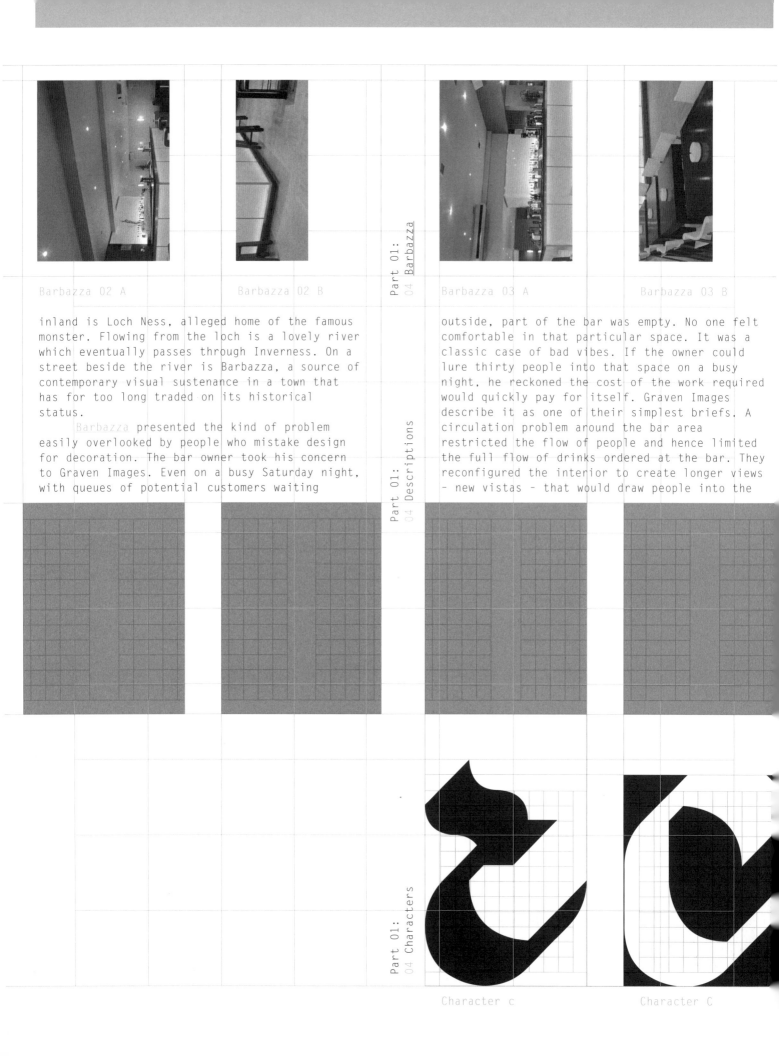

Barbazza 02 A

Barbazza 02 B

Barbazza 03 A

Barbazza 03 B

inland is Loch Ness, alleged home of the famous monster. Flowing from the loch is a lovely river which eventually passes through Inverness. On a street beside the river is Barbazza, a source of contemporary visual sustenance in a town that has for too long traded on its historical status.

Barbazza presented the kind of problem easily overlooked by people who mistake design for decoration. The bar owner took his concern to Graven Images. Even on a busy Saturday night, with queues of potential customers waiting

outside, part of the bar was empty. No one felt comfortable in that particular space. It was a classic case of bad vibes. If the owner could lure thirty people into that space on a busy night, he reckoned the cost of the work required would quickly pay for itself. Graven Images describe it as one of their simplest briefs. A circulation problem around the bar area restricted the flow of people and hence limited the full flow of drinks ordered at the bar. They reconfigured the interior to create longer views - new vistas - that would draw people into the

Character c

Character C

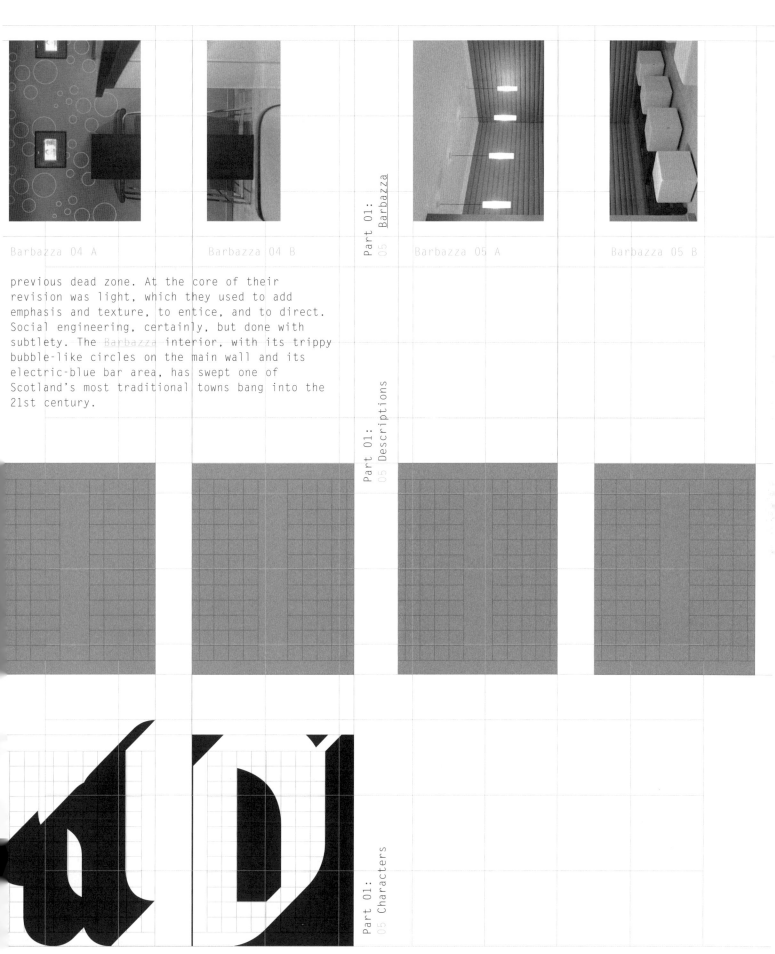

Barbazza 04 A

Barbazza 04 B

Barbazza 05 A

Barbazza 05 B

previous dead zone. At the core of their
revision was light, which they used to add
emphasis and texture, to entice, and to direct.
Social engineering, certainly, but done with
subtlety. The Barbazza interior, with its trippy
bubble-like circles on the main wall and its
electric-blue bar area, has swept one of
Scotland's most traditional towns bang into the
21st century.

Character d

Character D

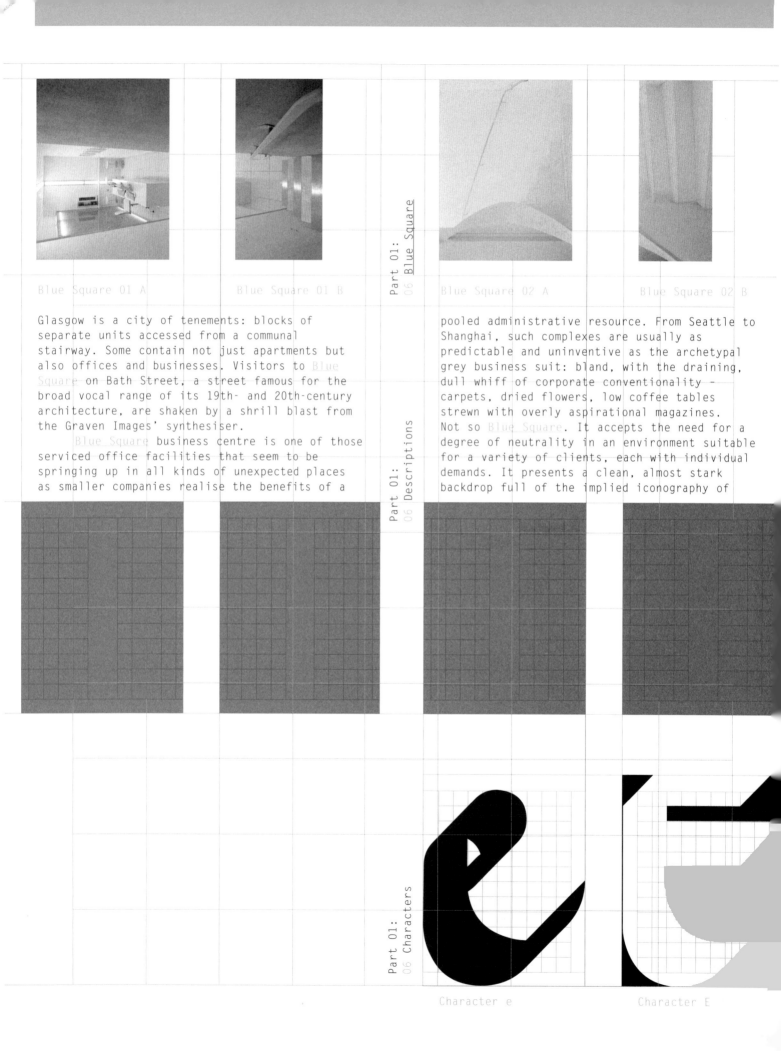

Blue Square 01 A   Blue Square 01 B   Blue Square 02 A   Blue Square 02 B

Glasgow is a city of tenements: blocks of separate units accessed from a communal stairway. Some contain not just apartments but also offices and businesses. Visitors to Blue Square on Bath Street, a street famous for the broad vocal range of its 19th- and 20th-century architecture, are shaken by a shrill blast from the Graven Images' synthesiser.

Blue Square business centre is one of those serviced office facilities that seem to be springing up in all kinds of unexpected places as smaller companies realise the benefits of a

pooled administrative resource. From Seattle to Shanghai, such complexes are usually as predictable and uninventive as the archetypal grey business suit: bland, with the draining, dull whiff of corporate conventionality – carpets, dried flowers, low coffee tables strewn with overly aspirational magazines. Not so Blue Square. It accepts the need for a degree of neutrality in an environment suitable for a variety of clients, each with individual demands. It presents a clean, almost stark backdrop full of the implied iconography of

Character e   Character E

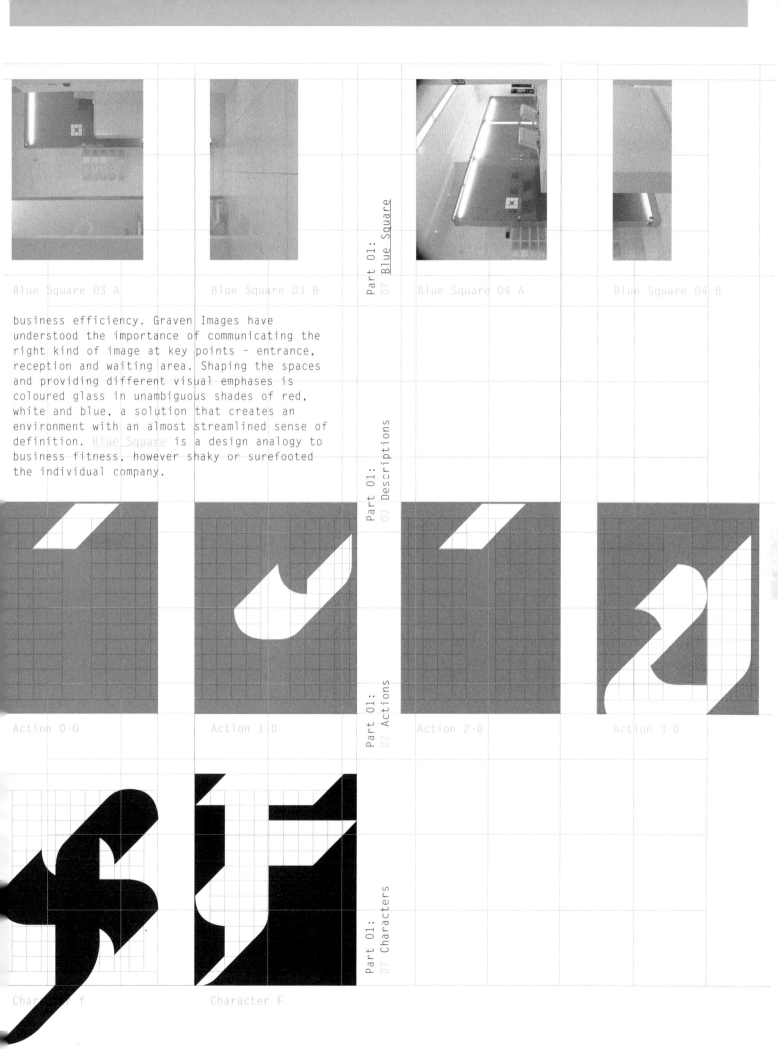

Blue Square 03 A

Blue Square 03 B

Blue Square 04 A

Blue Square 04 B

business efficiency. Graven Images have
understood the importance of communicating the
right kind of image at key points - entrance,
reception and waiting area. Shaping the spaces
and providing different visual emphases is
coloured glass in unambiguous shades of red,
white and blue, a solution that creates an
environment with an almost streamlined sense of
definition. Blue Square is a design analogy to
business fitness, however shaky or surefooted
the individual company.

Action 0-0

Action 1-0

Action 2-0

Action 3-0

Character f

Character F

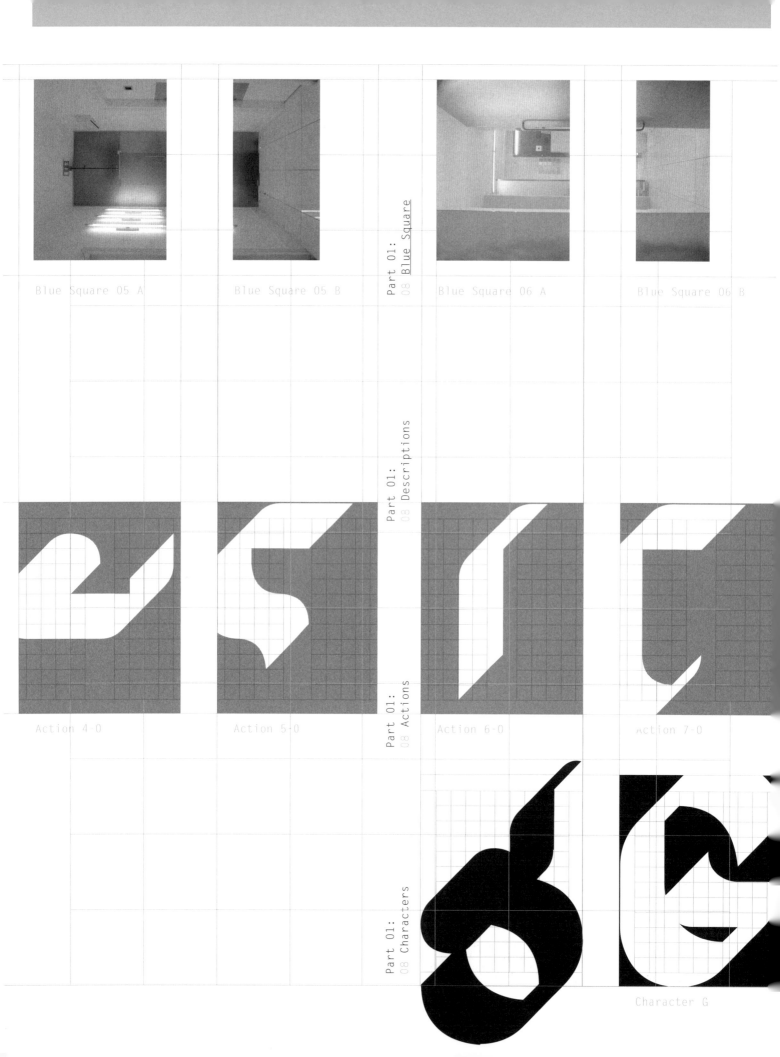

Blue Square 05 A

Blue Square 05 B

Blue Square 06 A

Blue Square 06 B

Action 4 0

Action 5 0

Action 6 0

Action 7 0

Character G

Cube 01

Cube 02

Cube 03

Cube 04

Set inside an industrial building in Musselburgh, a small town on the outskirts of Edinburgh, is one of Graven Images' cooler interiors. Cube marks an important point on their visual compass, and one of which Dan Flavin - the American guru of 'light as an art form' - would surely approve. Glass and light. These are the simple ingredients that Graven Images have configured to create a complex but understated series of spaces, a form of almost sculptural layering which turns an inarticulate shell into a place of endless potential for

personal and impersonal interaction. Cube is a club whose central 'enclosure' is the focus for music and dancing. Here people can react to each other directly. An abundance of peripheral space welcomes other activities. Strange and unexpected views are packed with endless opportunities for clubbers to ponder their individual roles in relation to the theatre going on around them. In comparison with some of Graven Images' earlier works, which deliberately tended towards overstatement, Cube is grown-up - a totally adult piece of design that accepts the intrinsic

Action 8-0

Action 9-0

Action 0-1

Action 1-1

Character h

Character H

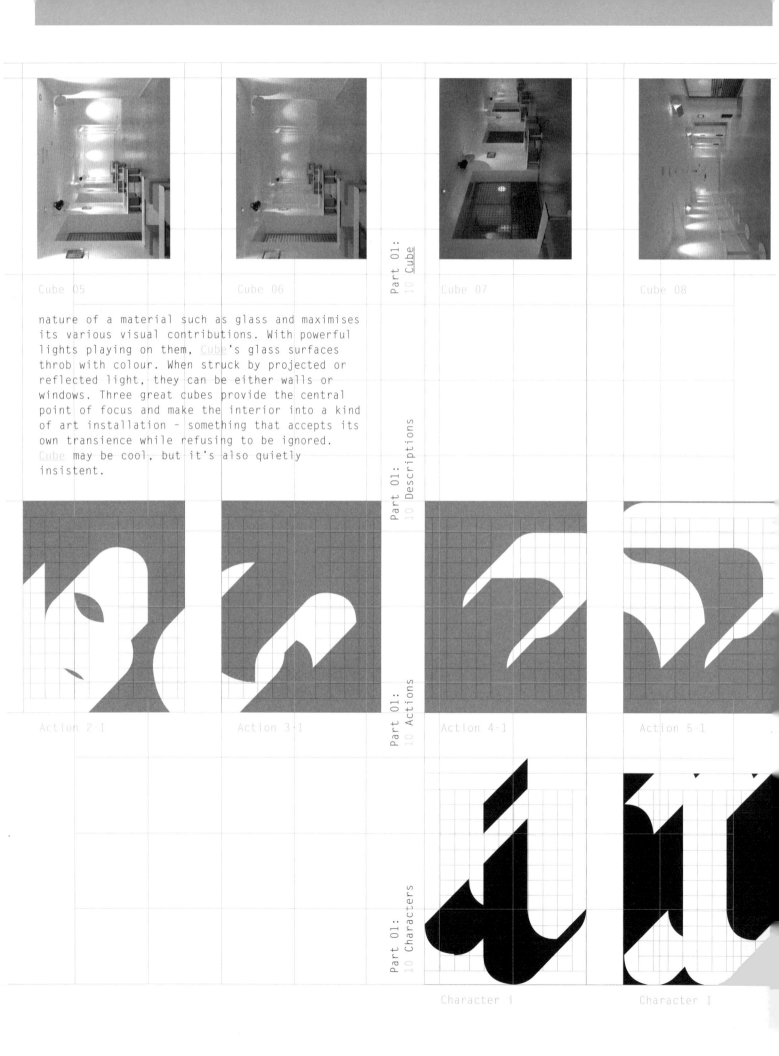

Cube 05

Cube 06

Cube 07

Cube 08

nature of a material such as glass and maximises
its various visual contributions. With powerful
lights playing on them, Cube's glass surfaces
throb with colour. When struck by projected or
reflected light, they can be either walls or
windows. Three great cubes provide the central
point of focus and make the interior into a kind
of art installation - something that accepts its
own transience while refusing to be ignored.
Cube may be cool, but it's also quietly
insistent.

Action 2-1

Action 3-1

Action 4-1

Action 5-1

Character i

Character I

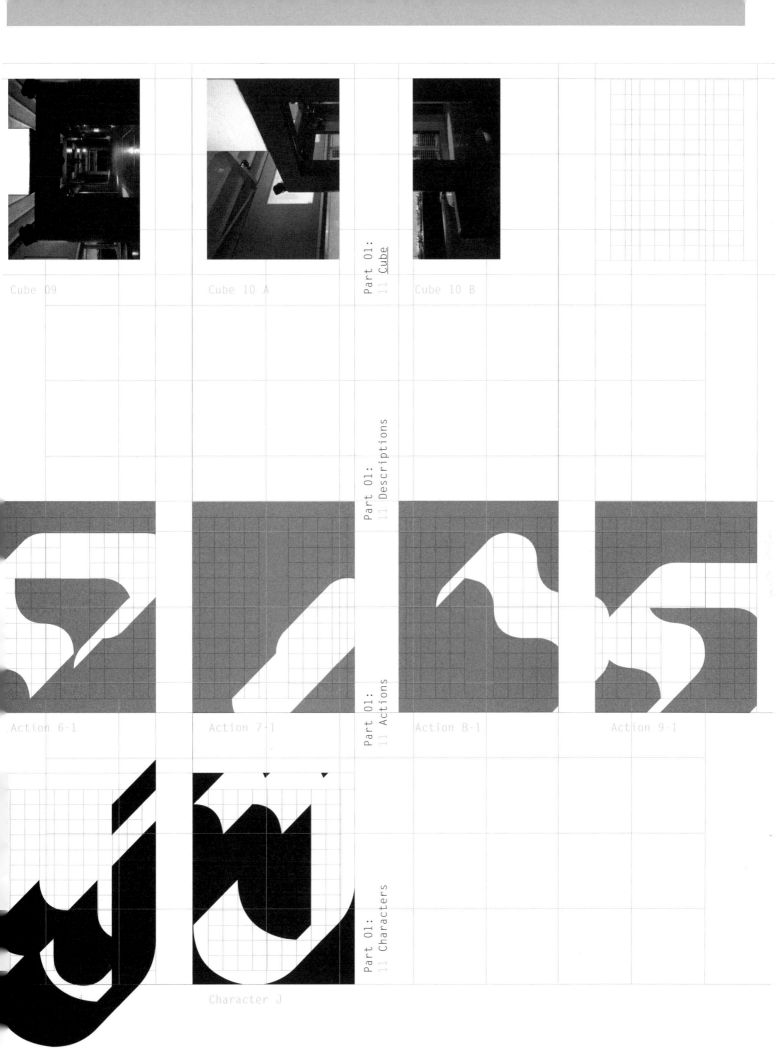

Cube 09

Cube 10 A

Cube 10 B

Part 01:
11 Descriptions

Part 01:
11 Actions

Action 6-1

Action 7-1

Action 8-1

Action 9-1

Part 01:
11 Characters

Character J

The Living Room 01   The Living Room 02

The Living Room 03 A   The Living Room 03 B

Nearly ten years on, it's hard to imagine the
enormous impact that this bar interior had on
Glasgow when it opened in 1993. Little more than
three months passed from commission to creation,
and within another three months pale replicas
were sprouting up all over the city.

    Graven Images have described it as 'camp
agricultural'. They used a bizarre if not
contradictory range of materials, setting a bar
front made of rubble that might have been a
section of wall from a Highland field next to
the most expensive French velour wallpaper Graven

Images could source. Tables made by local artist
Andy Scott and bent metal chairs – picture
Parisian café furniture on acid – accompanied
elements found in an architectural salvage yard.
Exposed brickwork and a distinctively Scottish
form of external weatherproofing – wet-dash
harling – made for a novel interior finish, while
agricultural string was used for the toilet
signs.

    The design was easily misunderstood. For
Graven Images, the project was a knowing sojourn
into the land of kitsch, a self-conscious

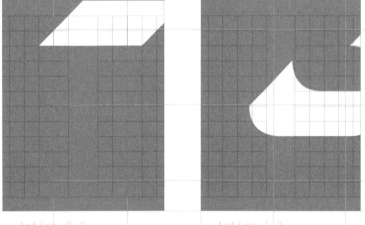

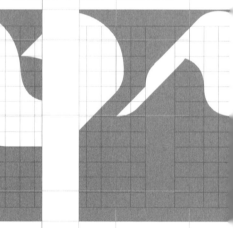

Action 0-2   Action 1-2

Action 2-2   Action 3-2

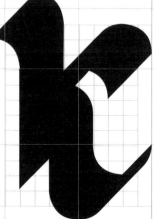
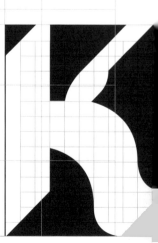

Character k   Character K

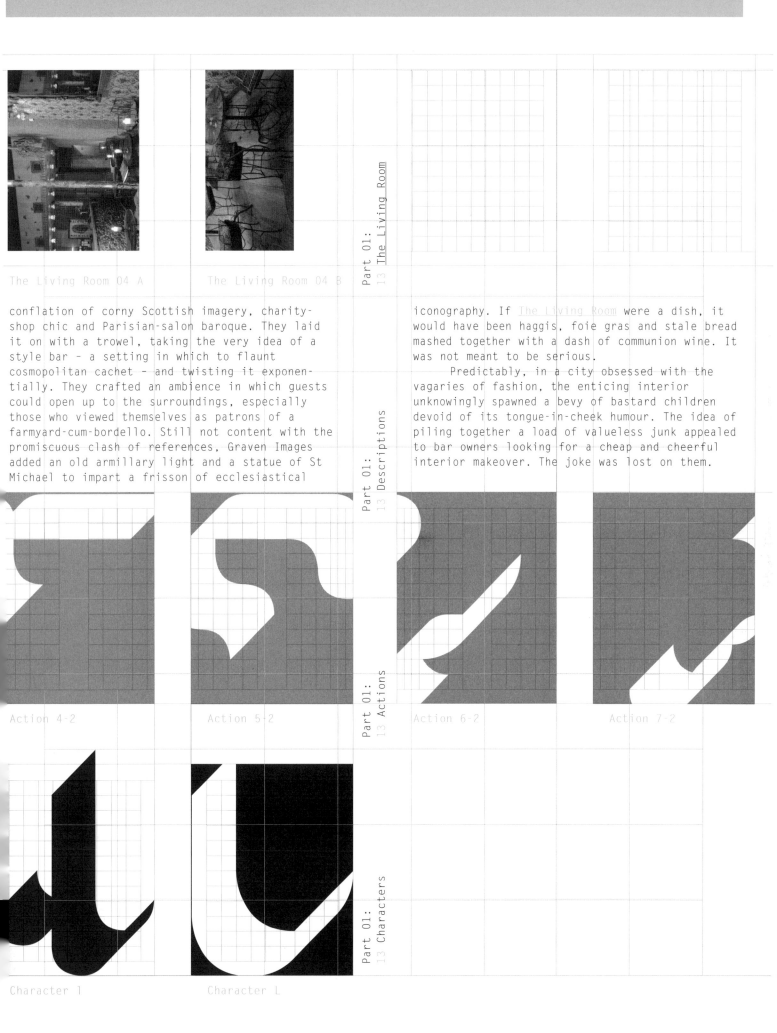

The Living Room 04 A

The Living Room 04 B

conflation of corny Scottish imagery, charity-shop chic and Parisian-salon baroque. They laid it on with a trowel, taking the very idea of a style bar - a setting in which to flaunt cosmopolitan cachet - and twisting it exponentially. They crafted an ambience in which guests could open up to the surroundings, especially those who viewed themselves as patrons of a farmyard-cum-bordello. Still not content with the promiscuous clash of references, Graven Images added an old armillary light and a statue of St Michael to impart a frisson of ecclesiastical

iconography. If The Living Room were a dish, it would have been haggis, foie gras and stale bread mashed together with a dash of communion wine. It was not meant to be serious.

Predictably, in a city obsessed with the vagaries of fashion, the enticing interior unknowingly spawned a bevy of bastard children devoid of its tongue-in-cheek humour. The idea of piling together a load of valueless junk appealed to bar owners looking for a cheap and cheerful interior makeover. The joke was lost on them.

Action 4-2

Action 5-2

Action 6-2

Action 7-2

Character 1

Character L

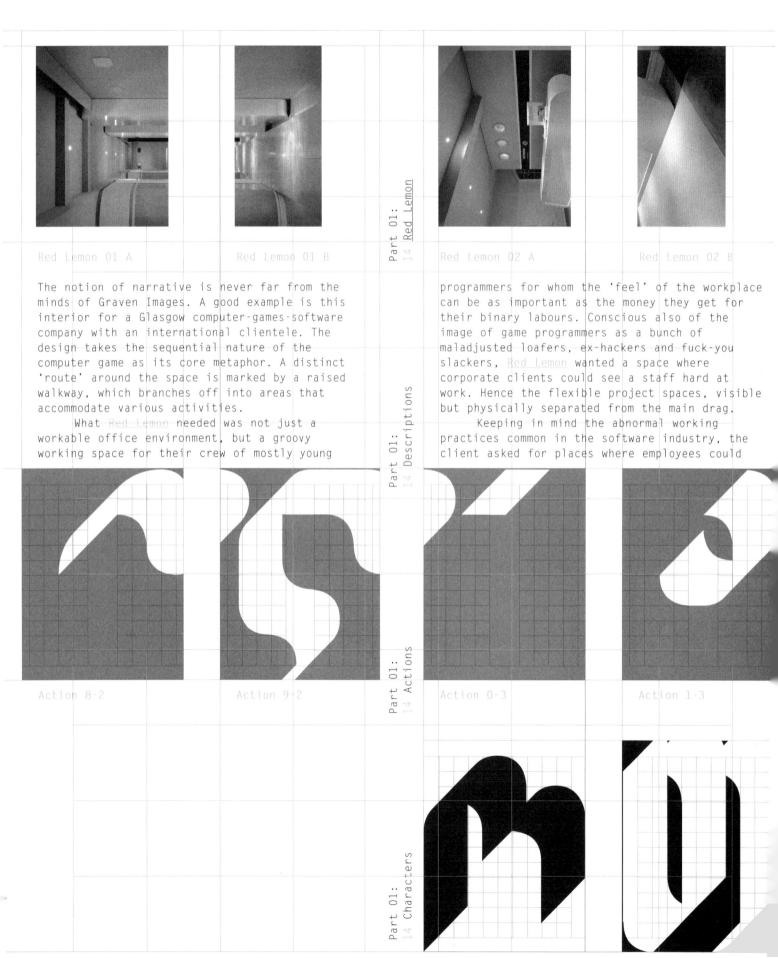

Red Lemon 01 A

Red Lemon 01 B

Red Lemon 02 A

Red Lemon 02 B

The notion of narrative is never far from the minds of Graven Images. A good example is this interior for a Glasgow computer-games-software company with an international clientele. The design takes the sequential nature of the computer game as its core metaphor. A distinct 'route' around the space is marked by a raised walkway, which branches off into areas that accommodate various activities.

What Red Lemon needed was not just a workable office environment, but a groovy working space for their crew of mostly young programmers for whom the 'feel' of the workplace can be as important as the money they get for their binary labours. Conscious also of the image of game programmers as a bunch of maladjusted loafers, ex-hackers and fuck-you slackers, Red Lemon wanted a space where corporate clients could see a staff hard at work. Hence the flexible project spaces, visible but physically separated from the main drag.

Keeping in mind the abnormal working practices common in the software industry, the client asked for places where employees could

Action 8-2

Action 9-2

Action 0-3

Action 1-3

Character m

Character M

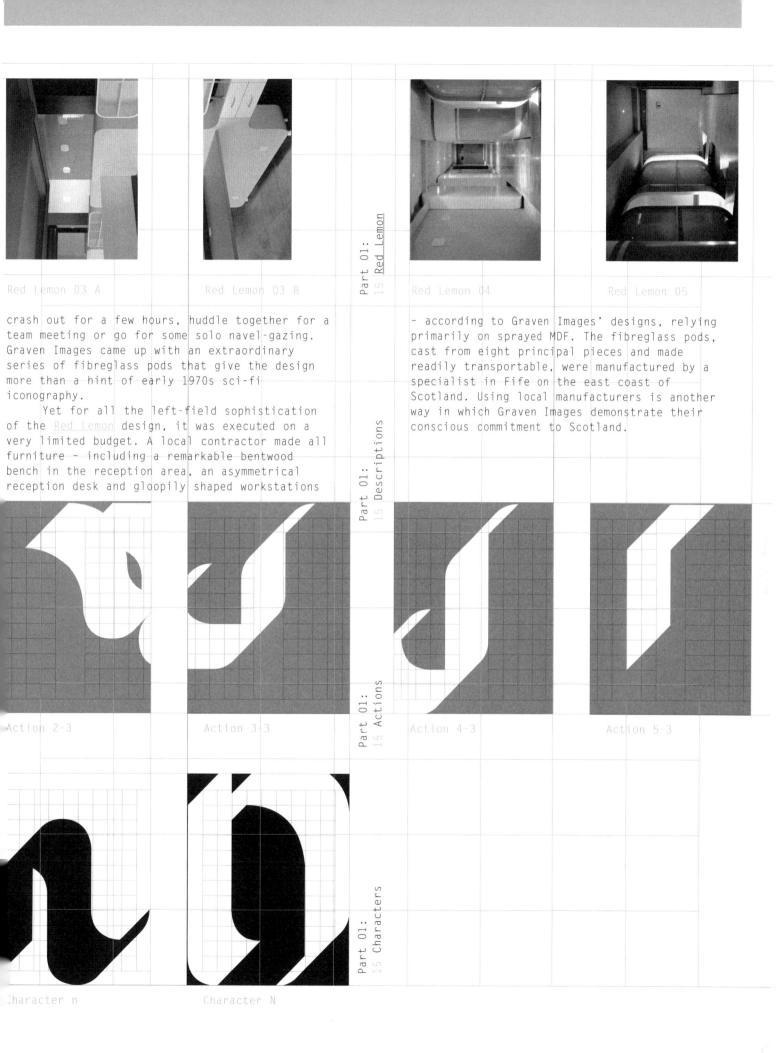

Red Lemon 03 A

Red Lemon 03 B

Red Lemon 04

Red Lemon 05

crash out for a few hours, huddle together for a team meeting or go for some solo navel-gazing. Graven Images came up with an extraordinary series of fibreglass pods that give the design more than a hint of early 1970s sci-fi iconography.

Yet for all the left-field sophistication of the Red Lemon design, it was executed on a very limited budget. A local contractor made all furniture - including a remarkable bentwood bench in the reception area, an asymmetrical reception desk and gloopily shaped workstations

- according to Graven Images' designs, relying primarily on sprayed MDF. The fibreglass pods, cast from eight principal pieces and made readily transportable, were manufactured by a specialist in Fife on the east coast of Scotland. Using local manufacturers is another way in which Graven Images demonstrate their conscious commitment to Scotland.

Action 2-3

Action 3-3

Action 4-3

Action 5-3

Character n

Character N

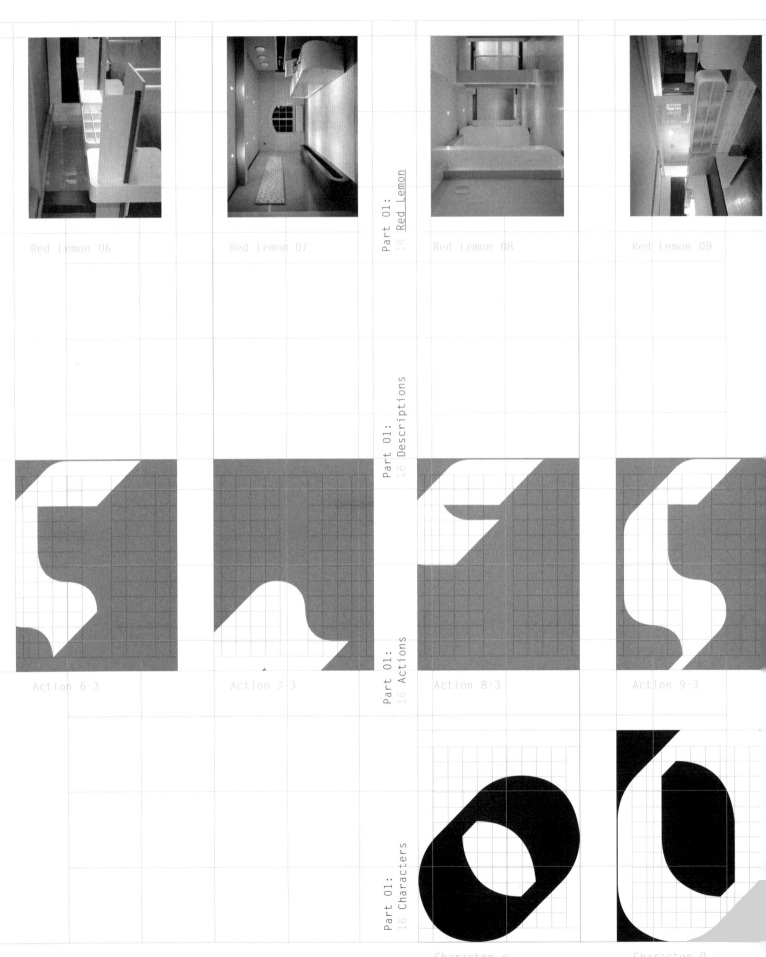

Red Lemon 06

Red Lemon 07

Part 01:
16 Red Lemon

Red Lemon 08

Red Lemon 09

Part 01:
16 Descriptions

Action 6-3

Action 7-3

Part 01:
16 Actions

Action 8-3

Action 9-3

Part 01:
16 Characters

Character o

Character 0

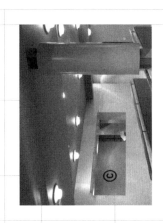

Room at the Top 01

Room at the Top 02

Room at the Top 03

Room at the Top 04 A

A nightclub for 200 can be a simple box, but one built to accommodate over 2000 people demands some serious thought. Although situated in the rather nondescript Scottish town of Bathgate, Room at the Top is one of Britain's larger nightclubs, a venue that represents Graven Images' sound understanding of social engineering and crowd control.

Laid out on a roughly triangular plan with a curved extension, the building was presented to Graven Images largely as an empty canvas. The picture they have conjured up is vibrant,

composed and richly rewarding. It uses different aspects of design to get clubbers circulating throughout the building, while avoiding bottlenecks and their potentially negative consequences. Most internal partition walls are set at unexpected angles, creating a sense of formal unpredictability. Rounded forms meet linear ones pretty much head-on. Large, open areas for dancing are complemented by smaller, quieter, more enclosed places that invite guests to chat, drink and look around.

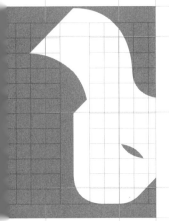

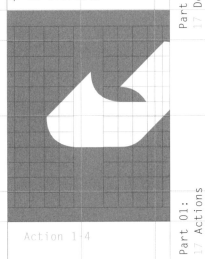

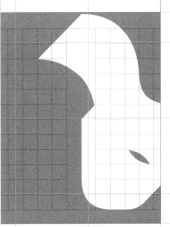

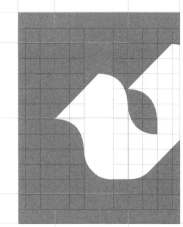

Action 0-4

Action 1-4

Action 2-4

Action 3-4

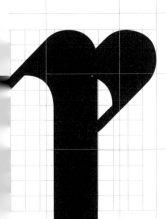

Charact

Character P

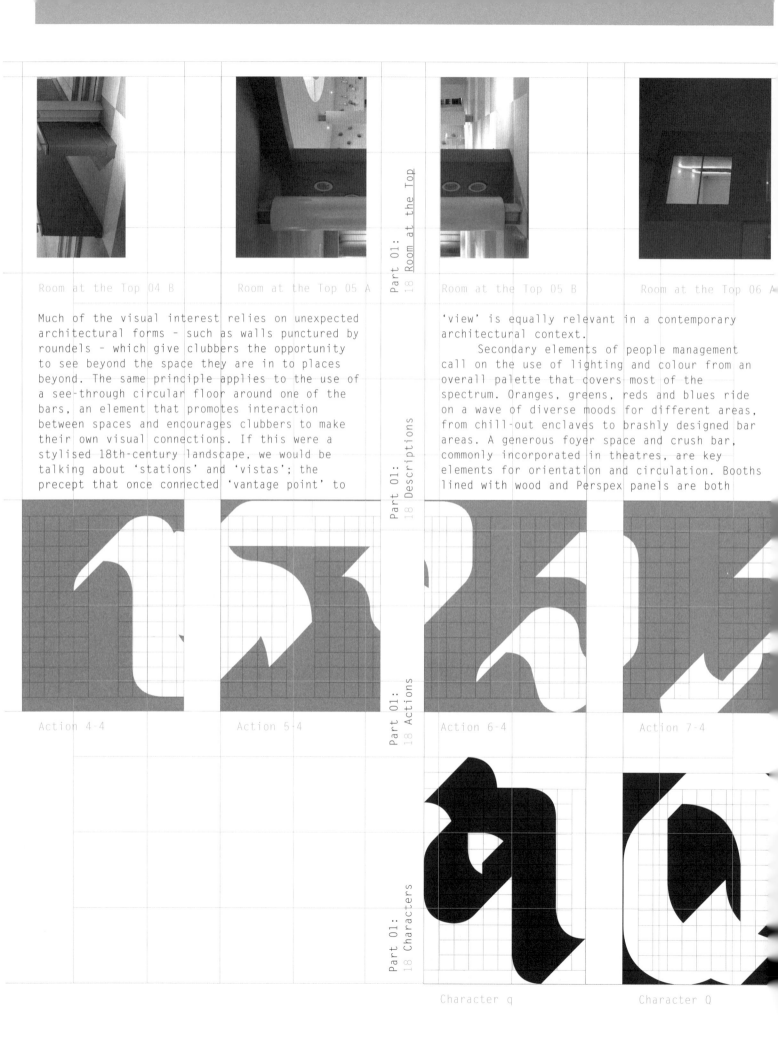

Room at the Top 04 B

Room at the Top 05 A

Room at the Top 05 B

Room at the Top 06 A

Much of the visual interest relies on unexpected
architectural forms – such as walls punctured by
roundels – which give clubbers the opportunity
to see beyond the space they are in to places
beyond. The same principle applies to the use of
a see-through circular floor around one of the
bars, an element that promotes interaction
between spaces and encourages clubbers to make
their own visual connections. If this were a
stylised 18th-century landscape, we would be
talking about 'stations' and 'vistas'; the
precept that once connected 'vantage point' to

'view' is equally relevant in a contemporary
architectural context.

Secondary elements of people management
call on the use of lighting and colour from an
overall palette that covers most of the
spectrum. Oranges, greens, reds and blues ride
on a wave of diverse moods for different areas,
from chill-out enclaves to brashly designed bar
areas. A generous foyer space and crush bar,
commonly incorporated in theatres, are key
elements for orientation and circulation. Booths
lined with wood and Perspex panels are both

Action 4-4

Action 5-4

Action 6-4

Action 7-4

Character q

Character Q

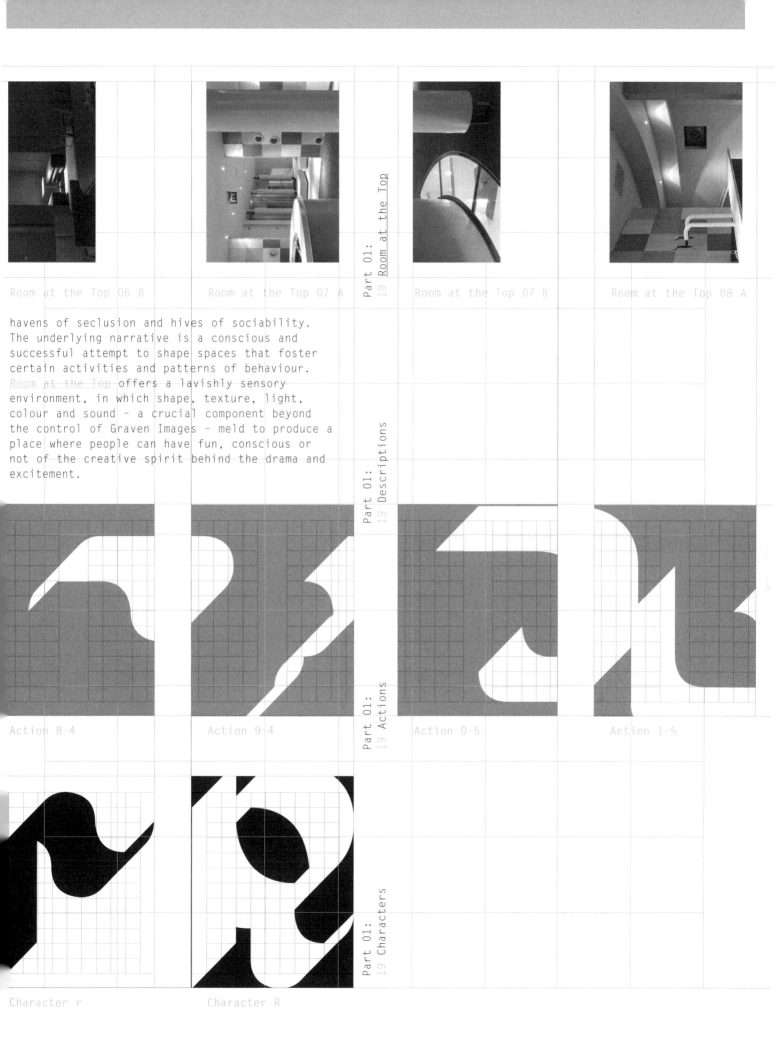

Room at the Top 06 B   Room at the Top 07 A   Room at the Top 07 B   Room at the Top 08 A

havens of seclusion and hives of sociability.
The underlying narrative is a conscious and
successful attempt to shape spaces that foster
certain activities and patterns of behaviour.
Room at the Top offers a lavishly sensory
environment, in which shape, texture, light,
colour and sound - a crucial component beyond
the control of Graven Images - meld to produce a
place where people can have fun, conscious or
not of the creative spirit behind the drama and
excitement.

Action 8-4   Action 9-4   Action 0-5   Action 1-5

Character r   Character R

Room at the Top 08 B

Room at the Top 09

Room at the Top 10

Room at the Top 11

Action 2-5

Action 3-5

Action 4-5

Action 5-5

Character s

Character S

Room at the Top 12

Room at the Top 13

Room at the Top 14

Room at the Top 15

Action 6-5

Action 7-5

Action 8-5

Action 9-5

Character t

Character T

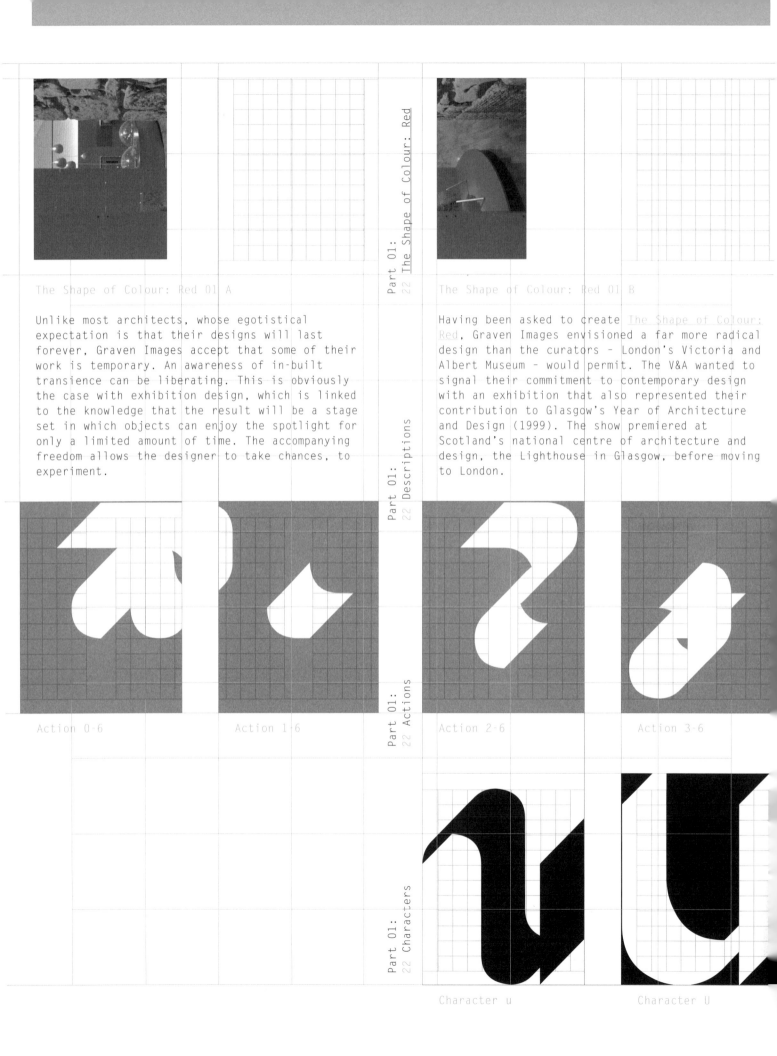

The Shape of Colour: Red 01 A

Unlike most architects, whose egotistical
expectation is that their designs will last
forever, Graven Images accept that some of their
work is temporary. An awareness of in-built
transience can be liberating. This is obviously
the case with exhibition design, which is linked
to the knowledge that the result will be a stage
set in which objects can enjoy the spotlight for
only a limited amount of time. The accompanying
freedom allows the designer to take chances, to
experiment.

The Shape of Colour: Red 01 B

Having been asked to create The Shape of Colour:
Red, Graven Images envisioned a far more radical
design than the curators - London's Victoria and
Albert Museum - would permit. The V&A wanted to
signal their commitment to contemporary design
with an exhibition that also represented their
contribution to Glasgow's Year of Architecture
and Design (1999). The show premiered at
Scotland's national centre of architecture and
design, the Lighthouse in Glasgow, before moving
to London.

Action 0-6

Action 1-6

Action 2-6

Action 3-6

Character u

Character U

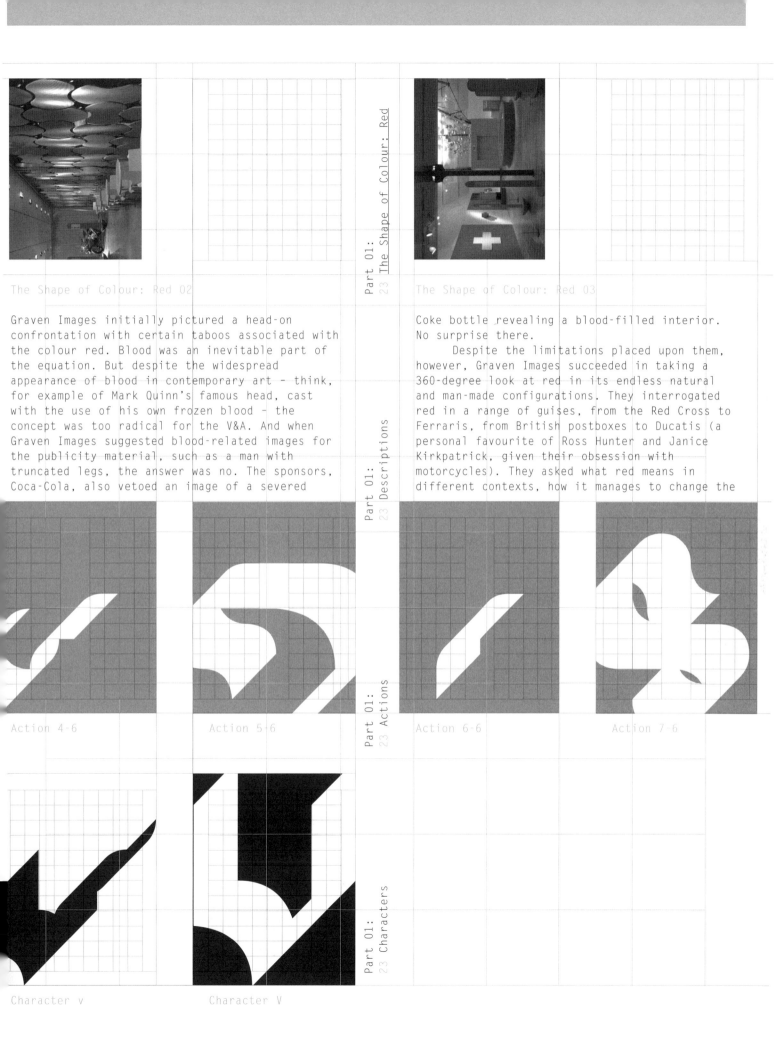

The Shape of Colour: Red 02

The Shape of Colour: Red 03

Graven Images initially pictured a head-on
confrontation with certain taboos associated with
the colour red. Blood was an inevitable part of
the equation. But despite the widespread
appearance of blood in contemporary art – think,
for example of Mark Quinn's famous head, cast
with the use of his own frozen blood – the
concept was too radical for the V&A. And when
Graven Images suggested blood-related images for
the publicity material, such as a man with
truncated legs, the answer was no. The sponsors,
Coca-Cola, also vetoed an image of a severed

Coke bottle revealing a blood-filled interior.
No surprise there.
    Despite the limitations placed upon them,
however, Graven Images succeeded in taking a
360-degree look at red in its endless natural
and man-made configurations. They interrogated
red in a range of guises, from the Red Cross to
Ferraris, from British postboxes to Ducatis (a
personal favourite of Ross Hunter and Janice
Kirkpatrick, given their obsession with
motorcycles). They asked what red means in
different contexts, how it manages to change the

Action 4-6

Action 5-6

Action 6-6

Action 7-6

Character v

Character V

values attributed to different objects, how its
meaning can alter with such variation, and how
it acts as a warning mechanism. They integrated
shape, form and colour in a display that made
text itself one of the exhibits, encompassing
viewers and allowing them to participate in and
interact with their surroundings. Here made
manifest was the Graven Images conception of
text as a 'container for language'.

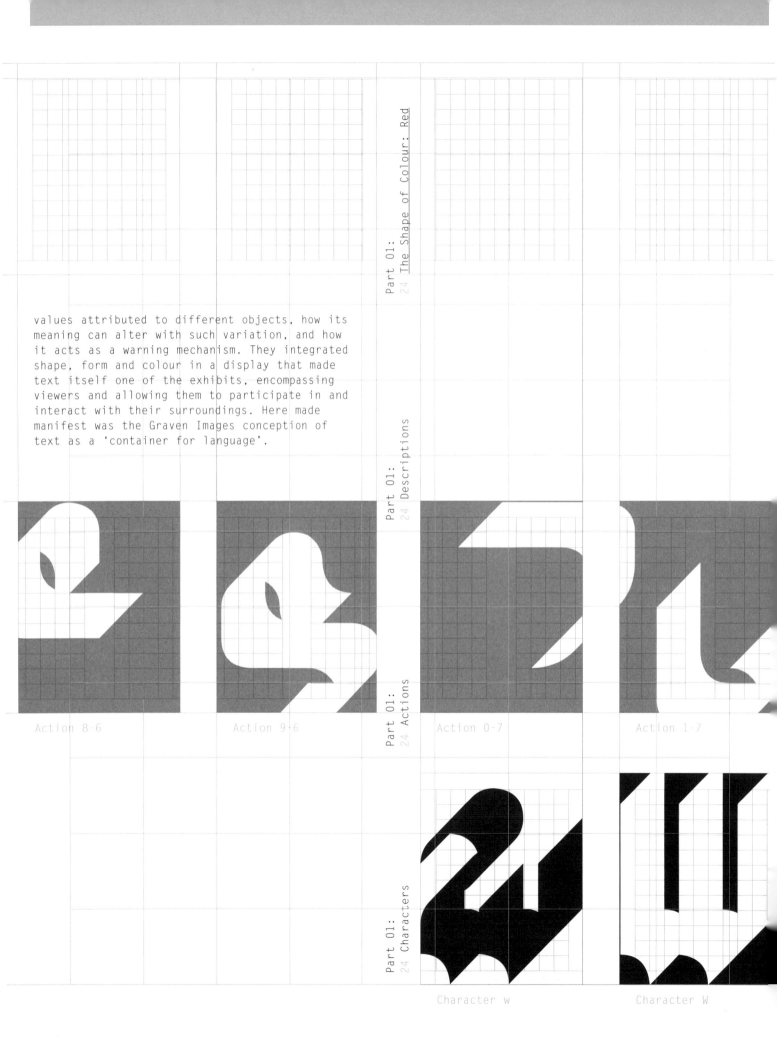

Action 8-6

Action 9-6

Action 0-7

Action 1-7

Character W

Character W

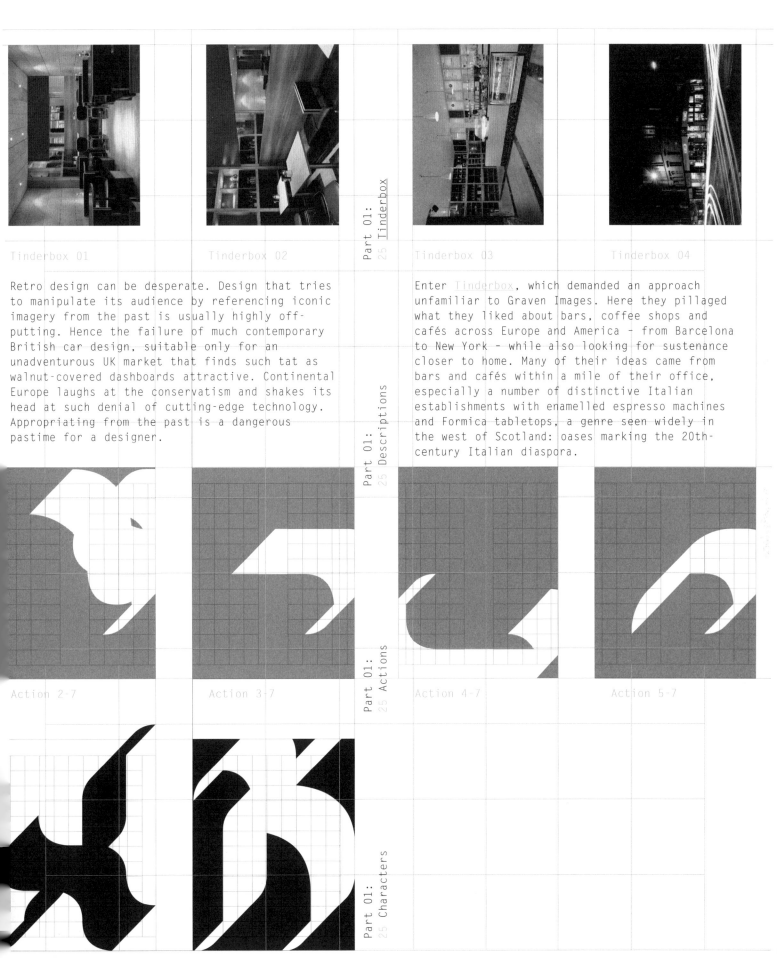

Tinderbox 01

Tinderbox 02

Tinderbox 03

Tinderbox 04

Retro design can be desperate. Design that tries to manipulate its audience by referencing iconic imagery from the past is usually highly off-putting. Hence the failure of much contemporary British car design, suitable only for an unadventurous UK market that finds such tat as walnut-covered dashboards attractive. Continental Europe laughs at the conservatism and shakes its head at such denial of cutting-edge technology. Appropriating from the past is a dangerous pastime for a designer.

Enter Tinderbox, which demanded an approach unfamiliar to Graven Images. Here they pillaged what they liked about bars, coffee shops and cafés across Europe and America - from Barcelona to New York - while also looking for sustenance closer to home. Many of their ideas came from bars and cafés within a mile of their office, especially a number of distinctive Italian establishments with enamelled espresso machines and Formica tabletops, a genre seen widely in the west of Scotland: oases marking the 20th-century Italian diaspora.

Action 2-7

Action 3-7

Action 4-7

Action 5-7

Character x

Character X

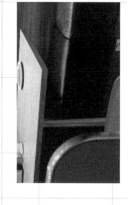

Tinderbox 05 A   Tinderbox 05 B

Tinderbox 06 A   Tinderbox 06 B

But where Graven Images succeed is in not being
too literal. The interiors of Tinderbox Glasgow
and Tinderbox London are more timeless than
retro; their gunmetal and red backdrops speak of
today as well as yesterday. They also show a
much-neglected but crucial distinction between
superficial design purely for retail purposes
and a deeper, more thoughtful approach that
accepts the potential of design to create rich
social spaces. Hence the small area at the back
of Tinderbox Glasgow, designed for cagey types -
schoolgirls bunking classes to sneak a

cigarette, or couples with good reason to keep
their relationship out of the public gaze. And
while the clandestine huddle behind the scenes,
exhibitionists perch on stools set at large
windows facing the street. Sipping their coffee,
they can scan the flow of passers-by and
traffic, and vice versa. For the eavesdropper,
there are the rows of back-to-back fixed seats -
perfect places to listen in on nearby
conversations. Introspection, interaction and
intrigue rub elbows in the same ecumenical,
democratic space. In the Tinderboxes - the

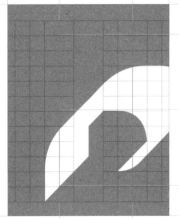

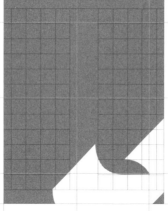

Action 6-7   Action 7-7   Action 8-7   Action 9-7

Character   Character Y

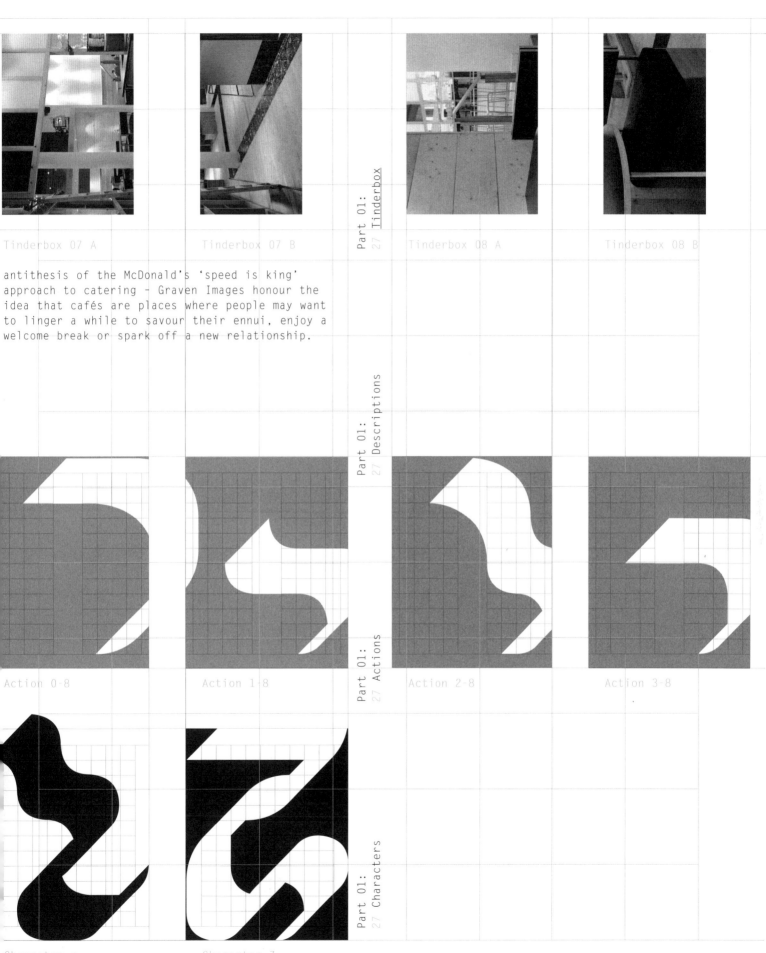

Tinderbox 07 A   Tinderbox 07 B

Part 01:
27 Tinderbox

Tinderbox 08 A   Tinderbox 08 B

antithesis of the McDonald's 'speed is king'
approach to catering – Graven Images honour the
idea that cafés are places where people may want
to linger a while to savour their ennui, enjoy a
welcome break or spark off a new relationship.

Part 01:
27 Descriptions

Part 01:
27 Actions

Action 0-8   Action 1-8   Action 2-8   Action 3-8

Part 01:
27 Characters

Character z   Character Z

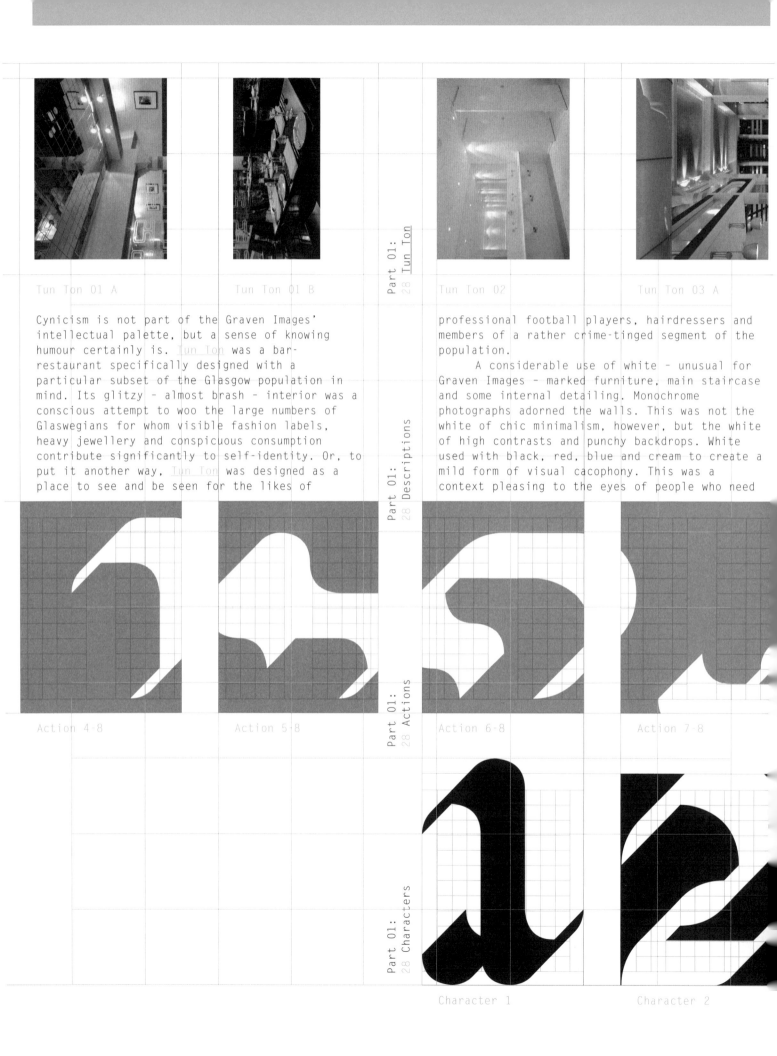

Tun Ton 01 A

Tun Ton 01 B

Tun Ton 02

Tun Ton 03 A

Cynicism is not part of the Graven Images'
intellectual palette, but a sense of knowing
humour certainly is. Tun Ton was a bar-
restaurant specifically designed with a
particular subset of the Glasgow population in
mind. Its glitzy - almost brash - interior was a
conscious attempt to woo the large numbers of
Glaswegians for whom visible fashion labels,
heavy jewellery and conspicuous consumption
contribute significantly to self-identity. Or, to
put it another way, Tun Ton was designed as a
place to see and be seen for the likes of

professional football players, hairdressers and
members of a rather crime-tinged segment of the
population.

A considerable use of white - unusual for
Graven Images - marked furniture, main staircase
and some internal detailing. Monochrome
photographs adorned the walls. This was not the
white of chic minimalism, however, but the white
of high contrasts and punchy backdrops. White
used with black, red, blue and cream to create a
mild form of visual cacophony. This was a
context pleasing to the eyes of people who need

Action 4-8

Action 5-8

Action 6-8

Action 7-8

Character 1

Character 2

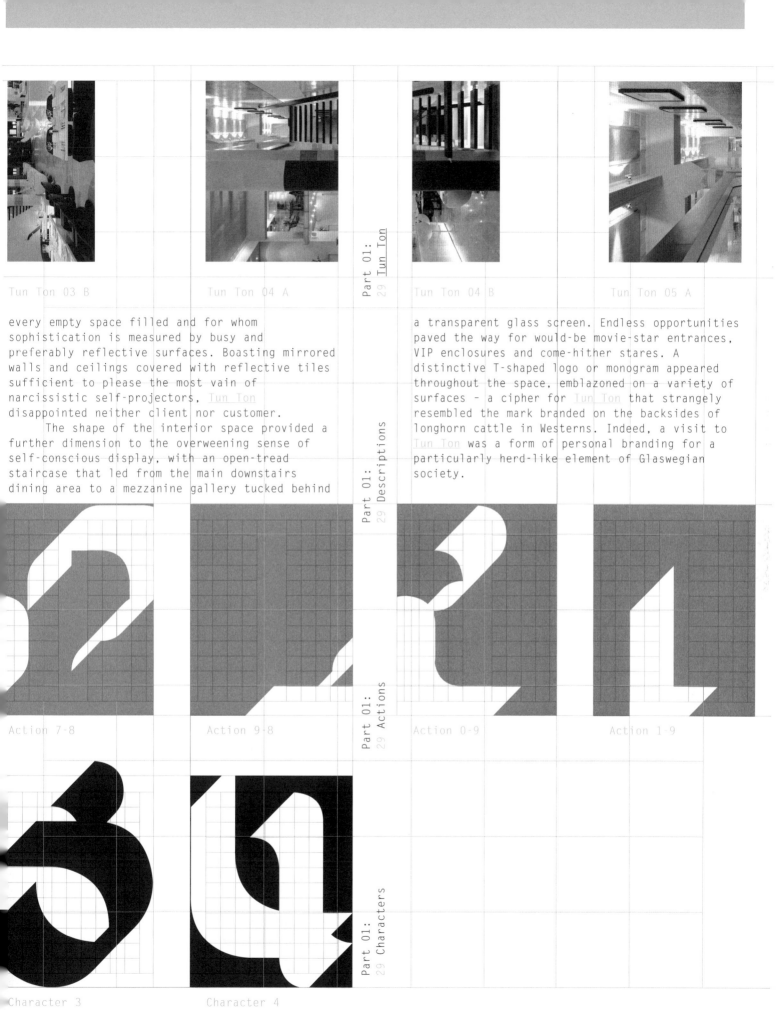

Tun Ton 03 B

Tun Ton 04 A

Tun Ton 04 B

Tun Ton 05 A

every empty space filled and for whom
sophistication is measured by busy and
preferably reflective surfaces. Boasting mirrored
walls and ceilings covered with reflective tiles
sufficient to please the most vain of
narcissistic self-projectors, Tun Ton
disappointed neither client nor customer.

The shape of the interior space provided a
further dimension to the overweening sense of
self-conscious display, with an open-tread
staircase that led from the main downstairs
dining area to a mezzanine gallery tucked behind

a transparent glass screen. Endless opportunities
paved the way for would-be movie-star entrances,
VIP enclosures and come-hither stares. A
distinctive T-shaped logo or monogram appeared
throughout the space, emblazoned on a variety of
surfaces - a cipher for Tun Ton that strangely
resembled the mark branded on the backsides of
longhorn cattle in Westerns. Indeed, a visit to
Tun Ton was a form of personal branding for a
particularly herd-like element of Glaswegian
society.

Action 7-8

Action 9-8

Action 0-9

Action 1-9

Character 3

Character 4

Tun Ton 05 B

Action 2-9

Action 3-9

Part 01:
30 Actions

Action 4-9

Action 5-9

Part 01:
30 Characters

Character 5

Character 6

Action 6-9

Action 7-9

Part 01:
31 Actions

Action 8-9

Action 9-9

Part 01:
31 Characters

Character 7

Character 8

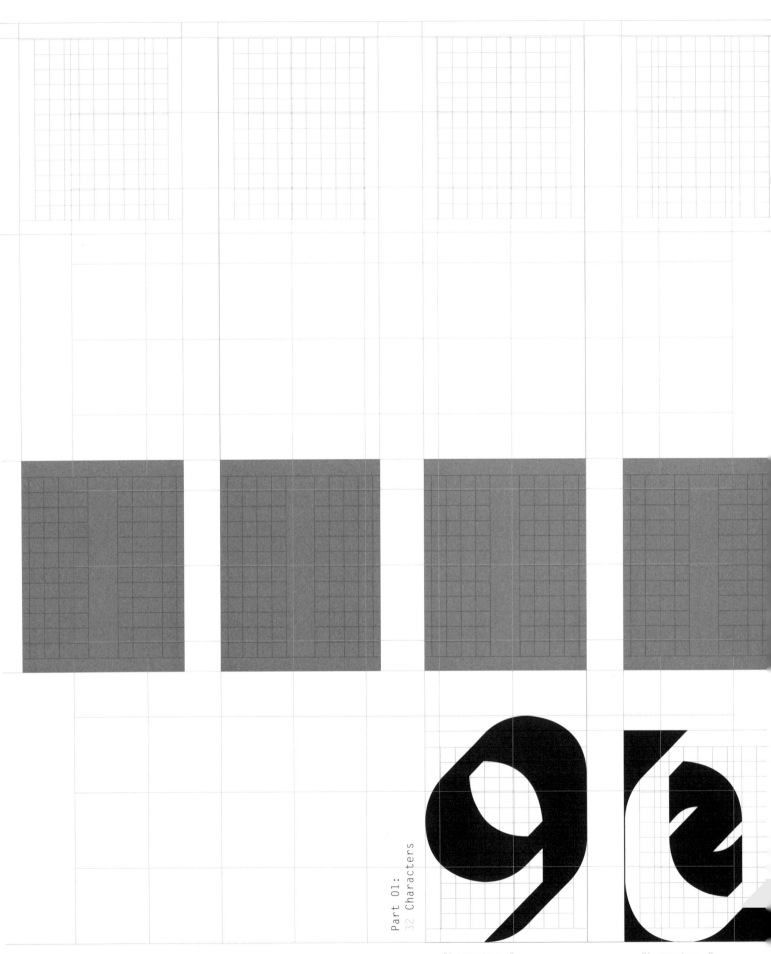

Part 01:
32 Characters

Scotland. A country on the geographical periphery of Europe. England's northern neighbour. Tartan. Mountains. Castles. Whisky. Forget these stereotypes. Someone once described Scotland as a semiconductor country, and not just because of the major employment now provided by the computer industry. Scotland's history is written in a binary code of duality and contradiction. It should be no surprise that the greatest novel to deal with the idea of split personality, <u>The Strange Case of Dr Jekyll and Mr Hyde</u>, was written by Robert Louis Stevenson, a Scotsman. Tartan was a Victorian invention. Most of Scotland's population live not in a rural setting but in an industrial belt stretching from the west coast to the east. Excluding the old Eastern bloc, Glasgow has the largest amount of social housing in Europe. The country has one of the worst rates of alcohol-related deaths in Europe, and Glasgow has more intravenous drug users than the rest of the UK, including London, put together.

Historically, Scotland has always had close ties to the Continent. As far back as the 12th century, French religious foundations were finding their way to Scottish shores. Legend has it that the

Scottish king presented a unicorn horn to the greatest ecclesiastic in Europe outside of Rome: Abbot Suger of the French royal church at St Denis near Paris. A peculiar combination of pragmatism and fantasy has long been a Scottish trait. In the 16th century the Renaissance reached Scotland before arriving in London, bringing with it architecture designed and built by masons brought directly from the French court. After all, the Scottish king, James V, had taken the daughter of King Francis of France as his wife. Scotland's two main cities - Edinburgh on the east coast and Glasgow on the west - compete with each other. Glasgow is bigger, but Edinburgh is the capital. Glasgow is a classic example of post industrialism, while Edinburgh benefits from being the centre of government, recently devolved from London. Edinburgh retains its medieval and neoclassical character, but Glasgow, considered in the 18th century to be one of the more beautiful cities in Europe, blasted itself apart in the industrialisation of the 19th century and again in the modernist idealism of the 1960s.

A city with an aggressive culture of religious conflict - typified by its football teams, Celtic and Rangers - Glasgow is also one of the most unselfconsciously cultured and design-conscious places in Europe. Fashion is a principal mechanism by which a fascination with design is expressed, with personal display being a crucial defining element in the lives of a large proportion of its declining population. Glasgow obviously thrives on the interaction of collectivist culture and personal branding.

This is also a city with an immense and impressive history in art, architecture and engineering. Glasgow has a venerable 13th-century cathedral which rivals the grand churches of continental Europe, world-class 19th-century buildings and the honour of having spawned a brilliantly innovative architect and designer, Charles Rennie Mackintosh, whose Glasgow School of Art ranks as one of the seminal buildings of the 20th century. The city's tradition in heavy engineering, typified by the vast number of ships built in its yards in the 19th and early 20th centuries, formerly had no equal.

Glasgow, once known as the second city of the British Empire, now has some of the worst social problems - including unemployment, drug abuse and poor housing - of any city in the UK. Yet despite all the negativity, Glasgow is still one of the great cities of the world, a place with an attitude open to outside influences, a flourishing artistic community that seems to thrive on adversity, and some of the better young design companies and architects in Europe. It is in Glasgow that Graven Images have been based since they were formed.

AGAINST THE GRAIN

True to the traditionally collectivist ethos of Scottish culture, Graven Images present themselves as a company of about fifteen people - just about the size of a football team plus substitutes. Of course, all have their own specialisms, and the structure of the office is defiantly non-hierarchical, but key decisions are taken by the company's two founders, Ross Hunter and Janice Kirkpatrick, without whom Graven Images would not exist. The pair established the company in 1985, having met while studying at Glasgow School of Art. Hunter and Kirkpatrick are Graven Images. Watching them in discussion brings to mind the power of creatively competitive relationships of the kind found in the world of music - Jagger and Richards of The Rolling Stones or Strummer and Jones of The Clash - relationships that feed on conflict and collaboration. What may come as a surprise is

that Hunter and Kirkpatrick are also partners in private life. Hunter studied architecture and Kirkpatrick graphic design. Their choices are key to the cross-disciplinary, pluralist approach to design that defines Graven Images - an awareness of the interconnectedness of two-dimensional and three-dimensional design that allows them to take on projects more specialised firms would never contemplate. They disregard the conventionally separate disciplines of architecture, interior design, exhibition design, graphic design and product design, refusing to accept the sort of creative and physical limitations that many others are forced to acknowledge.

In breadth of approach they are following a well-established tradition amongst Scottish designers. Mackintosh, for example, not only designed architecture, but also furniture and fittings for the interior spaces of his buildings. In the 19th century the great Glasgow-based architect Alexander 'Greek' Thomson also designed fittings for his own buildings, and another Scot, Robert Adam - the greatest British architect of the 18th century - inspired the 'Adam style', a comprehensive term applicable to both interior and furniture design. Graven Images are part of a distinguished Scottish tradition that avoids over-specialisation and celebrates a generalist policy. For Hunter and Kirkpatrick, however, the pluralist approach is rooted to some degree in adversity. Unlike many of their art-school contemporaries who followed the traditional Scottish diaspora, they stayed in Glasgow, resisting the easier option of journeying to London or abroad to further their careers by joining existing firms. They opted for the independence of having their own company, their own potential for failure or success. Not surprisingly, both partners are obsessed with high-performance motorcycles, being natural risk-takers who enjoy interrogating the parameters of the safety envelope. When they started the company, money was short. Undaunted by a second-rate office with filthy water dripping from the ceiling, they began by making things they could sell - furnishings such as mirrors faced with spikes. Ironically, given the biblical connotations of their name, one of their first commissions was to design a mosaic for a church. Although they had no work-related experience on which to rely, they took on the commission and the result was a success. They seized the opportunity and made the best of it. This pragmatic acceptance of the need to

respond to situations rather than to force their own agenda is another key element in defining what Graven Images are about. They are unpretentious professionals, unconcerned with narrow definitions of style and fashion, but conscious of the need for designs that satisfy the brief, the client, the audience and the designers themselves.

PROPS AND BACKDROPS
Looking back over the two decades that Graven Images have been in operation, one realises that much of their work has emerged from a specifically Glaswegian context. Like many industrial cities, Glasgow has long had a vibrant culture of bars, restaurants and nightclubs - an antidote to the drudgery of office or factory and a contrast to the limitations and privations of home. Places where ordinary people can transcend themselves, reinvent themselves, bask in a glamour missing from their everyday lives and alter the normal chemistry of their minds. Before the Second World War, it was cinemas and dance halls that provided the most immediate route to escapism. Since the 1960s in Glasgow, bars and nightclubs have filled this need, and it is in the design of such spaces that Graven Images have defined their

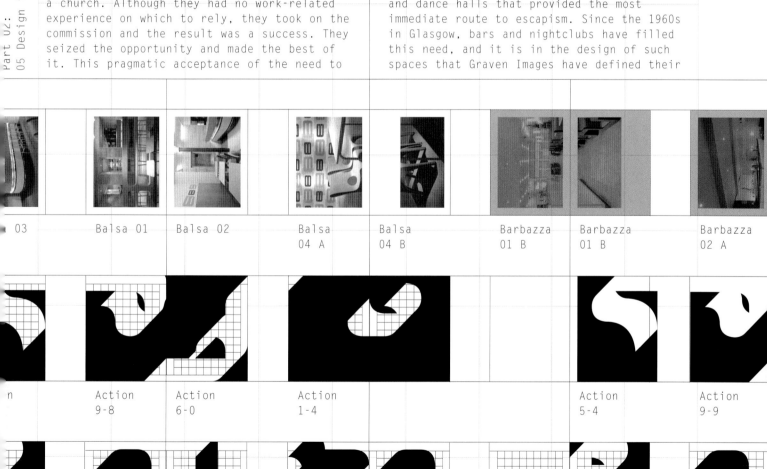

| 03 | Balsa 01 | Balsa 02 | Balsa 04 A | Balsa 04 B | Barbazza 01 B | Barbazza 01 B | Barbazza 02 A |

| n | Action 9-8 | Action 6-0 | Action 1-4 | | | Action 5-4 | Action 9-9 |

| cter | Character a | Character l | Character s | Character a | | Character B | Character a |

approach. As Hunter has said in another context, they have provided 'props and backdrops to give order to the chaotic drama of life's everyday theatre' - places where everyone is an actor in his or her own drama or tragedy. But there is another aspect to Graven Images, which seems at first to contradict their involvement with places of public entertainment. They have also done a number of design projects for the UK government through such organisations as The British Council - effectively the cultural arm of the Foreign Office. These have included international exhibitions on such diverse themes as football, the colour red, and Islam, the last having been opened by Her Majesty the Queen. Graven Images somehow manage to be establishment and anti-establishment at the same time, characteristics that have been defined in another context as reflecting a peculiarly Scottish idea of the 'democratic intellect'. As Kirkpatrick has pointed out, being a designer normally gets you boardroom-level access to a company, and Graven Images are as happy dealing with senior managers at IBM as they are with the owner of a Glasgow nightclub. It was in this spirit that they undertook the complete redesign of the respected Glasgow-based broadsheet, The Herald, discussing their ideas directly with the typesetters as well as with the management of the newspaper. And underlining her sense of the need to educate people as broadly as possible about design, Kirkpatrick has had her own critically acclaimed television series broadcast by the BBC, covering with a truly original perspective such varied but fundamental subjects as the wheel and the chair.

GLASWEGIAN PRAGMATISTS
One valuable by-product of the open-agenda, pragmatic approach to design taken by Graven Images is that they don't think of design purely in formal and visual terms. When dealing with interior spaces, they also understand, as all good architects must, that psychology is a key ingredient in a successful design - a design that people respond to positively. Ideas of progression, sequence, narrative and even hierarchy are all pertinent. Call it architectural ergonomics or even social engineering. Call it what you will. It works.

It appears in designs such as Room at the Top, a nightclub in the no-nonsense town of Bathgate in central Scotland, where a

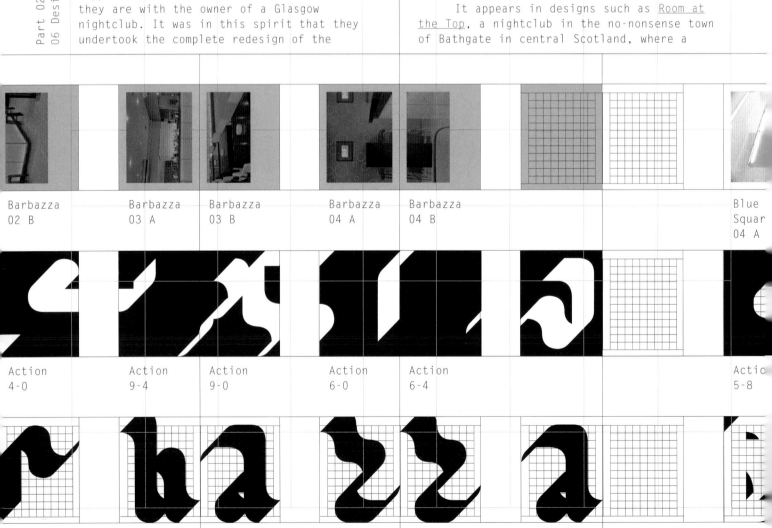

Barbazza 02 B	Barbazza 03 A	Barbazza 03 B	Barbazza 04 A	Barbazza 04 B	Blue Squar 04 A
Action 4-0	Action 9-4	Action 9-0	Action 6-0	Action 6-4	Actio 5-8
Character r	Character b	Character a	Character z	Character z	Character a	Chara B

series of interrelated but discrete (and sometimes discreet) spaces provides not only a sense of exploration and variety for clubbers, but also a practical means by which to guide and manage up to three thousand people safely. The plan was implemented with a sense of fun and imaginative visual flair, using such elements as walls punctured with roundels and see-through floors. The idea that interior design can be about open-ended narrative as well as static form was demonstrated in one of Graven Images' early make-overs: The Living Room, a bar in Glasgow. A mongrel crossover between kitsch Scottish self-mockery, Hellfire Club decadence and Parisian bistro accessibility, it made no attempt to disguise its falseness and contrivance. Envision if you will an architectural analogy to Brechtian theatre. Cheap to realise - a crucial factor - the design relied largely on material that was intrinsically worthless but visually valuable. Unsurprisingly, its immediate success gave rise to a host of imitators, and The Living Room soon appeared sadly out of date.

A quick decline into obsolescence might have been anticipated. Style bars respond to fashion with astonishing rapidity, and in a city like Glasgow, with so much competition between bars and pubs trying to attract fickle custom, novelty can be an important part of a successful mix.

Yet Graven Images also understand the power of tradition, and their atmospheric, timeless coffee bars - Favorit and Tinderbox - play cleverly on the imagery of American diners and Italian cafés. Tinderbox was also influenced by classic examples in Glasgow and in popular tourist towns along the west coast of Scotland. With their metal and wood surfaces and rich palettes of browns, reds, greys and blacks, Graven Images' café interiors turn a coffee break into an occasion or perhaps even an adventure. A sense of drama - or perhaps more accurately, a sense of potential drama - also pervades their design for the Glasgow restaurant Tun Ton, where aggressively split levels engender a deliberate play on the contrast between physical interconnectedness and division. With an awareness of the power of the past to inform the imagery of the present - think of samplers in music - they used early 1970s iconography allied to contemporary forms to create a self-consciously kitsch and overloaded evocation of sumptuous stylishness. Balsa, a low-budget renovation

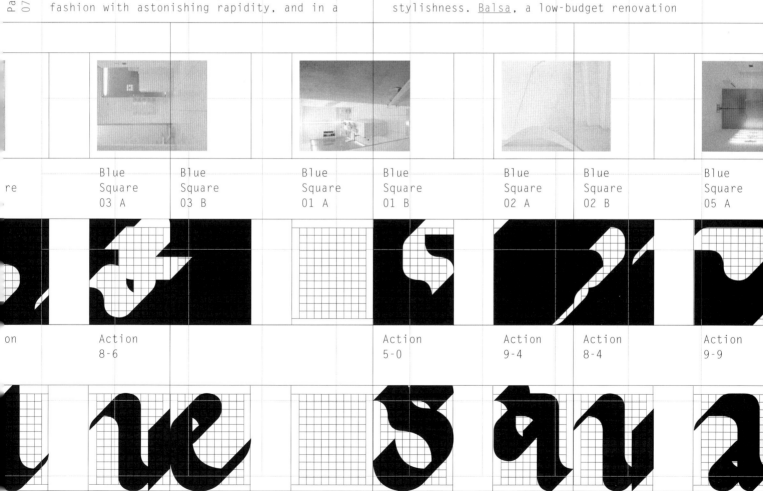

	Blue Square 03 A	Blue Square 03 B	Blue Square 01 A	Blue Square 01 B	Blue Square 02 A	Blue Square 02 B	Blue Square 05 A
on	Action 8-6			Action 5-0	Action 9-4	Action 8-4	Action 9-9
acter	Character u	Character e		Character S	Character q	Character u	Character a

of a Glasgow bar, boasts an array of colours - lime greens, maroons and blue-greys - made popular in the late 1960s by the great English textile designer Lucienne Day and here applied to the walls as vinyl graphics that provide simple but effective visual definition. For other projects, such as the Barbazza bar in Inverness in the Scottish Highlands, lighting that creates colour and visual emphasis, as well as illumination, turns a square space into an exciting physical environment. It would be wrong, however, to give the impression that Graven Images have a restricted repertoire. The Blue Square business centre in Glasgow shows their sensitivity to purpose by creating a precise, almost clinical aesthetic appropriate to an efficient commercial environment. Contrast this with their design for the offices of Red Lemon, a Glasgow-based outfit that designs games software, which must be one of the finest backdrops ever created for slackers in the process of turning themselves into serious businessmen. Part set for 2001: A Space Odyssey - complete with pod-shaped brainstorming/project/crash-out rooms - and part airport check-in desk circa 1973, the workplace even includes a sexually suggestive relief cast of cut lemons that would have

made Fornasetti proud. And with a provocatively understated colour scheme that features beige, cream and off-white, the design shows that Graven Images can easily alter their game when the parameters change. In many ways, the design for Red Lemon typifies everything Graven Images represent: adaptability, pragmatism, adventure, sensitivity and humour. And in Glasgow, of all these, humour surely tops the list.

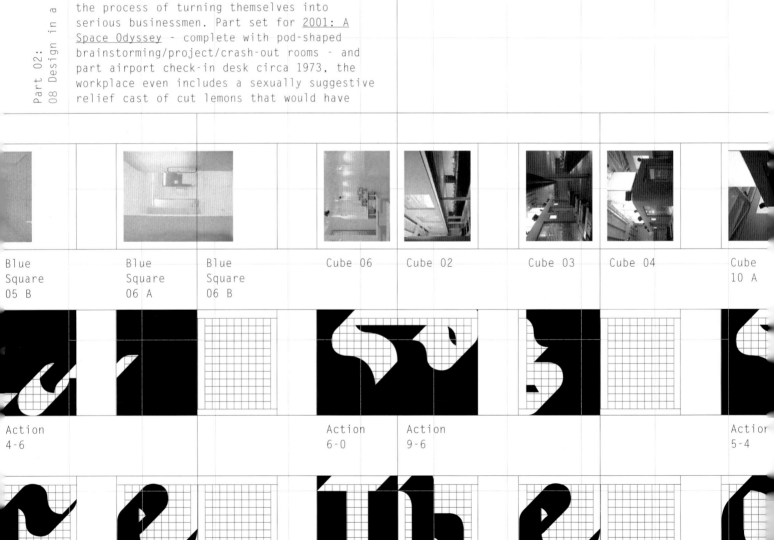

Blue Square 05 B
Blue Square 06 A
Blue Square 06 B
Cube 06
Cube 02
Cube 03
Cube 04
Cube 10 A

Action 4-6
Action 6-0
Action 9-6
Action 5-4

Character r
Character e
Character T
Character h
Character e
Character C

Cube 09

The Living
Room 01

The Living
Room 02

Action
9-6

Action
5-8

Action
6-6

Action
4-8

Action
6-9

Character
b

Character
e

Character
L

Character
i

Character
v

Character
i

FACE TO FACE WITH ROSS HUNTER AND
JANICE KIRKPATRICK

'Design is a process of controlling creativity. It's a way to understand and manipulate cultural elements like language, ritual and values.' This definition of design will not be the only one offered today by the verbally gifted founders of Graven Images, Janice Kirkpatrick and Ross Hunter. In fact, Kirkpatrick barely draws a breath before labelling design 'an inexact science, composed of intuition and underpinned with stolen methods' – adding, almost as an afterthought, 'but one that works'.

When I ask them to consider the phrase 'design in a cold climate', Kirkpatrick's response is a reference to her roots: 'The hardest part of designing in Scotland is the impossibility of removing myself from the ebb and flow of my own culture to see it more clearly.'

If familiarity represents such a stranglehold, why not leave? 'One of the reasons we set up the company in Glasgow,' says Hunter, 'is because we were told, as students, that staying here was taboo. It's still normal for staff at the Glasgow School of Art to suggest that the better students go to London or somewhere else. In Scotland, we still measure success by how well people do outside the country. Those who leave and make

The Living Room 03 A	The Living Room 03 B		The Living Room 04 A	The Living Room 04 B			Red L 02 A
Action 6-8				Action 6-5	Action 5-1	Action 5-9	
Character n		er g		Character R	Character o	Character o	Character m

their mark elsewhere are always considered to be more successful than those who stay here. Everyone was saying, "You can't do this." We faced the challenge by replying, "Let's see if we can." We certainly didn't imagine that we'd still be doing it sixteen or seventeen years later.'

Kirkpatrick continues to emphasise the downside of their decision, however. According to her, 'Scotland doesn't see the bigger picture - the need for infrastructure and the partnerships that can deliver it, the need for mentoring, development and investment that will strengthen our hand. We often can't tell the difference between riches and rubbish. We also confuse money and means.'

POLITICAL ACTIVITY
Criticism aside, it is this very environment that imbues their work with the distinctly Scottish sense of pragmatism so vital to their success. Hunter readily agrees. 'We've always mixed pragmatism and risk, but pragmatism has certainly been a driving force. If it were not for our pragmatic approach to design, we would not have survived. That cold climate you mentioned applies to Scotland in a commercial sense as

well. The country is economically moribund. And from a cultural point of view, although Glasgow certainly has an underlying appreciation of style, high design hasn't been a dominant part of the culture.'

Thoughts of pragmatism and a struggling economy prompt Kirkpatrick to come up with another definition of design, which she now refers to as 'a political activity'. She's convinced that the creative process is at least a partial solution to many of the issues facing society. 'It's important for cities, especially post-industrial cities, to use design as a tool for cultural change, as a framework with which to understand the archaeology of the past and to describe what the archaeology of the future might be. Glasgow knows that design can help to identify the real problems damaging Britain today. Homelessness, unemployment, drug abuse and lack of cultural identity are all symptoms of more deeply rooted problems, which politicians often tend to treat in merely tactical or superficial ways.'

'Glasgow has tried to transplant successful monolithic solutions from other cultures in a bid to solve its own problems,' she continues. 'These were doomed to failure, destroying confidence and the political will

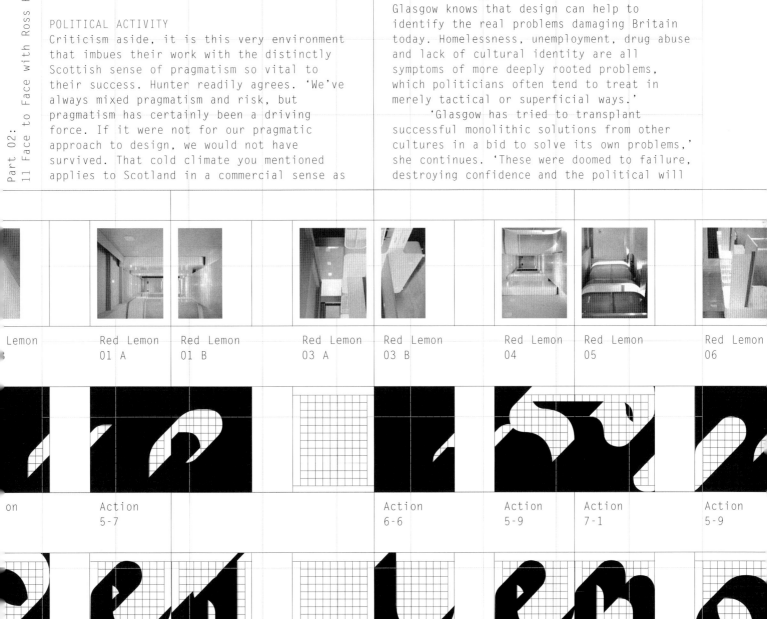

| Lemon | Red Lemon 01 A | Red Lemon 01 B | Red Lemon 03 A | Red Lemon 03 B | Red Lemon 04 | Red Lemon 05 | Red Lemon 06 |

| on | Action 5-7 | | | Action 6-6 | Action 5-9 | Action 7-1 | Action 5-9 |

| acter | Character e | Character d | | Character L | Character e | Character m | Character o |

to innovate and progress. Innovation requires deep self-knowledge, control and courage.' Kirkpatrick sees design not only as a remedy for society's ills, but also as a way to expose cultural differences and to express those features that make a place unique. Perhaps not unique, but fairly obvious, is the Glaswegian's tendency to equate style with something I like to call 'personal branding'. Nodding, Hunter suggests the term 'brash confidence' and says that it's an archetypal characteristic of the city's population. 'It warms the place up, makes it exciting, generates an air of vigour.' He turns a deaf ear to those who claim that only an inherent lack of confidence would make someone choose to be a walking advert for, say, Tommy Hilfiger or Gianni Versace. 'I don't think so,' is his simple reply.

GENUINE DIALOGUE

Leading the conversation away from culture, politics and Glaswegian gall, I ask them to tell me about another important but frequently ignored aspect of design: communication. Graven Images are known for dealing with everyone involved in a project – from managing director to joiner – on the same basis.

Hunter points out that communication is a two-way exercise. He talks about taking his technical drawing to the craftsman responsible for implementing the plan. 'It's not just me, the architect, telling the artisan what to do. The process starts with a conversation. Maybe he says, "I see what you're trying to do here, but we should make it slightly different." What follows is a genuine dialogue. The best craftsmen or builders understand what you're trying to do. Explaining to them the reason why is beneficial to both of you. It really helps if you outline the bigger idea. I don't just assume that the guy's a joiner and therefore doesn't really give a shit about why I want two pieces of wood to join back to front or whatever it is I have in mind. If I make him part of the process, he might contribute something worthwhile. Communication is important.' If the architect appreciates the drudgery involved in building the design, Hunter says, the artisan returns that appreciation with a job well done.

Kirkpatrick puts communication into a larger context. 'Architecture, art and design don't exist in a vacuum,' she asserts. 'Each is influenced by and expresses culture, economics and politics. Glasgow and Scotland

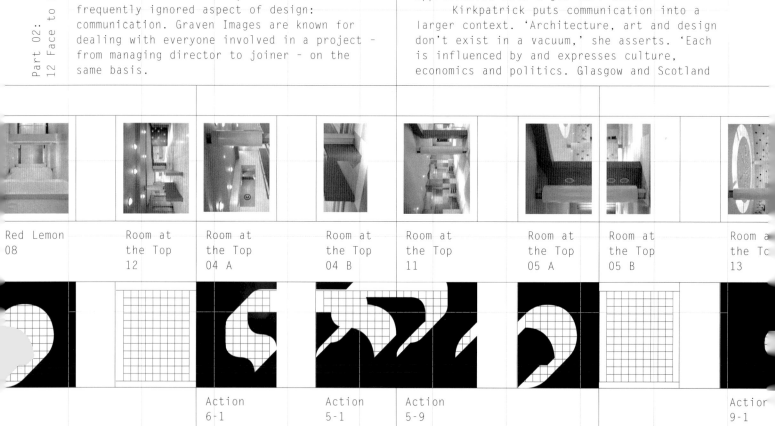

| Red Lemon 08 | Room at the Top 12 | Room at the Top 04 A | Room at the Top 04 B | Room at the Top 11 | Room at the Top 05 A | Room at the Top 05 B | Room at the Top 13 |

| | Action 6-1 | Action 5-1 | Action 5-9 | | | | Action 9-1 |

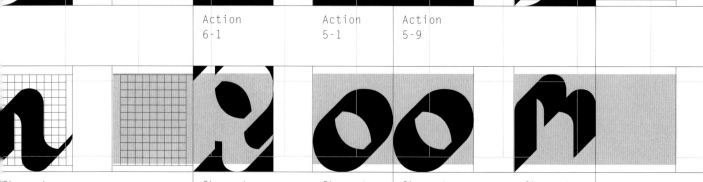

| Character n | | Character R | Character o | Character o | Character m | | Character a |

are learning to their cost the price of undervaluing the culture of a city and a nation.' They should see design as a tool for synthesis or reconstruction, she adds. 'Design can be used to acknowledge the past, to re-calibrate urban ideologies and to provide a framework for constructing an appropriate present and plans that will yield a future both familiar and new.'

Do the members of Graven Images ever think about design as an abstract concept? Hunter says they've entered competitions that revolved entirely around conceptual design. 'We did that scheme for Buchanan Street in Glasgow,' he reminds me, 'and we enjoyed the work. We've done retail projects that were all about concept as well, some of which were destined from the outset never to happen. They did exist for a reason, however. They helped move the client's brain from one place to another. Sometimes it's not necessary for a design to end as a finished product.'

STAGE SETS
Like many in Scotland's creative community, now and in the past, Graven Images are generalists rather than specialists. Hunter is convinced that specialisation goes hand in

hand with sterility. On the other hand, an excess of general knowledge can be detrimental to creativity. He'd like someone to 'draw a curve that would indicate the point at which knowledge starts to become counter-productive.' He's referring to the point at which 'too much information, too much knowledge or too much experience makes it difficult to take a fresh look at a project.' At the same time, he concedes, 'We are specialists in that we approach our work in a particular way. Because of our commitment to good communication – to the way in which spaces, things and objects communicate with the people that use them – our working methods have become second nature. And although I still think the old "form follows function" dictum is absolutely true, an object can have multiple functions that include something as trivial as making the user laugh.'

The laughter of a participating audience evokes images of the theatre, another strong link to the work of Graven Images, whose interior designs can often be compared to stage sets. I wonder aloud if they want to make spaces that invite users to reinvent their surroundings. 'When you create an interior or a space, you're inviting people

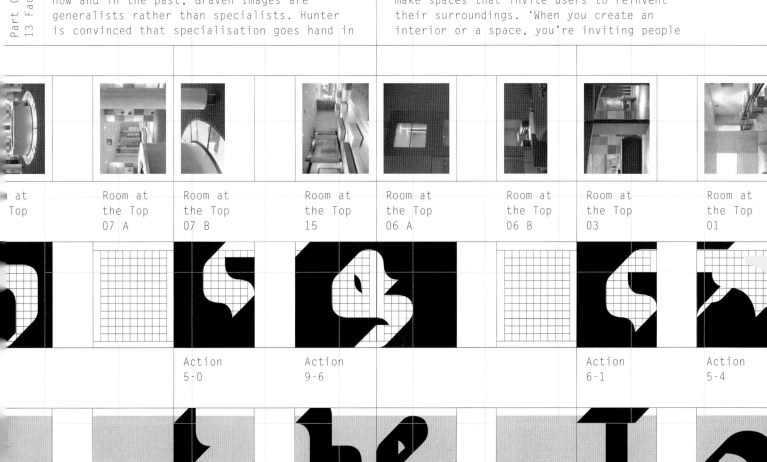

at Top	Room at the Top 07 A	Room at the Top 07 B	Room at the Top 15	Room at the Top 06 A	Room at the Top 06 B	Room at the Top 03	Room at the Top 01
	Action 5-0	Action 9-6			Action 6-1		Action 5-4
acter	Character t	Character h	Character e		Character T		Character o

to take part in something,' Hunter says. 'I'm always interested in what a subtle move or a minimal change will bring about. How will it affect the way people enter into the activity taking place within that space? The change can be really banal, like lowering the ceiling slightly. Will people sit down or remain standing? If we curve a wall, will visitors walk around it to see what's beyond the space?' He explains that his interest is more than simply formal. The theatricality of the designs is also a result of how Graven Images put the space together and of how they juxtapose materials to get a response from the user. The design is a spatial composition that has to 'work together'. The various elements cannot be treated separately. And nothing may be defined as 'two-dimensional', a term that Hunter describes as 'fatuous' in this context. 'The interior is not frozen in time,' he insists. 'Why, even a book is three-dimensional.'

Kirkpatrick backs him up. 'In recent years there's been an unfortunate tendency to factionalise design into different disciplines based on false notions of dimensionality - graphic design being forced into the two-dimensional category, for example, and product design and architecture

classified as three-dimensional.' She rejects the practice without exception.

MAKING PEOPLE LAUGH
In an attempt to take the topic of theatre a step further, I mention the iconography of projects like The Living Room and The Apartment, interior designs that transcend the generically designed environment thanks to a latent narrative. Hunter confirms the team's keen interest in narrative, but offers a different opinion with respect to The Living Room. 'That design is less about narrative than about our efforts to enliven a space by planting ideas in the minds of those occupying it. The way we dug into the texture of materials was aimed at reaching the individual. It was a highly formal game played with unlikely elements. Instead of using the materials and iconography associated with Barcelona's music bars at that time, we took our inspiration from objects that might be found in a rural skip or in the ruins of a sheep pen.'

The Living Room is not a 'theme bar', Hunter says adamantly, addressing a subject that makes his blood boil. 'Thematic design does exist, of course, but it's nothing more

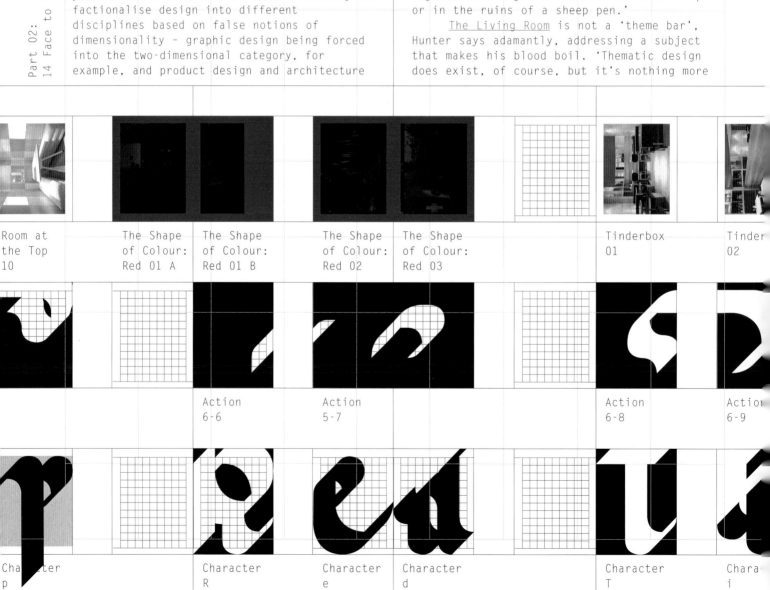

Room at the Top 10

The Shape of Colour: Red 01 A

The Shape of Colour: Red 01 B

The Shape of Colour: Red 02

The Shape of Colour: Red 03

Tinderbox 01

Tinder 02

Action 6-6

Action 5-7

Action 6-8

Action 6-9

Character p

Character R

Character e

Character d

Character T

Chara i

than a sleazy shortcut to an idea. It stunts the kind of real thinking that might lead to a good design.' The client who wants an interior 'with some sort of theme' would be wiser to take his business elsewhere. 'Putting a bunch of oriental or funfair objects into a space - or doing it up in '50s style, for example - doesn't do anything to me. It's completely flat.'

His partner points out that 'the intangible aspects of the design vocabulary are less obvious but more potent: smell, taste, touch, sound and temperature. They produce a frequently subliminal response and, when used intelligently, often defray the need for a tangible solution.'

When I mention the impossibility of reading a completely open-ended design like The Living Room in a literal way, Hunter replies that it wasn't supposed to be literal. 'We took an irreverent attitude towards the whole process of what was going on in bar design and, at the same time, gave it the measure of respect it deserved. The game involved the creation of something both sophisticated and crude.' The concept was sophisticated, the materialisation crude. Plastic string and corrugated iron topped a list of 'rural' attributes that gave

the designers the kitsch effect they were looking for.

The Living Room accepts its own contrivance, its own counterfeit nature. Rather than having an uncomfortable sense of being conned, visitors feel invited to take part in the joke. 'You can put material together in a way that makes people laugh,' says Hunter. 'Generally, people are quite sophisticated. They understand why something is funny or why something makes them feel one way or another. How it all fits together can evoke powerful emotions.' The distinction is a subtle one, but the humour he's talking about has nothing to do with wit. 'There's a certain postmodern conceit attached to wit, a certain Englishness. Whereas work that smiles rather than wisecracks lasts much longer. It's that kind of warmth that we try to achieve.'

QUALITY OF THOUGHT
'Designers must be inventive and structured in their thought process, which is essentially inductive,' interjects Kirkpatrick. She goes on to explain that after identifying the fundamental and dynamic forces within an organisation, the designer is responsible for making order of chaos, for

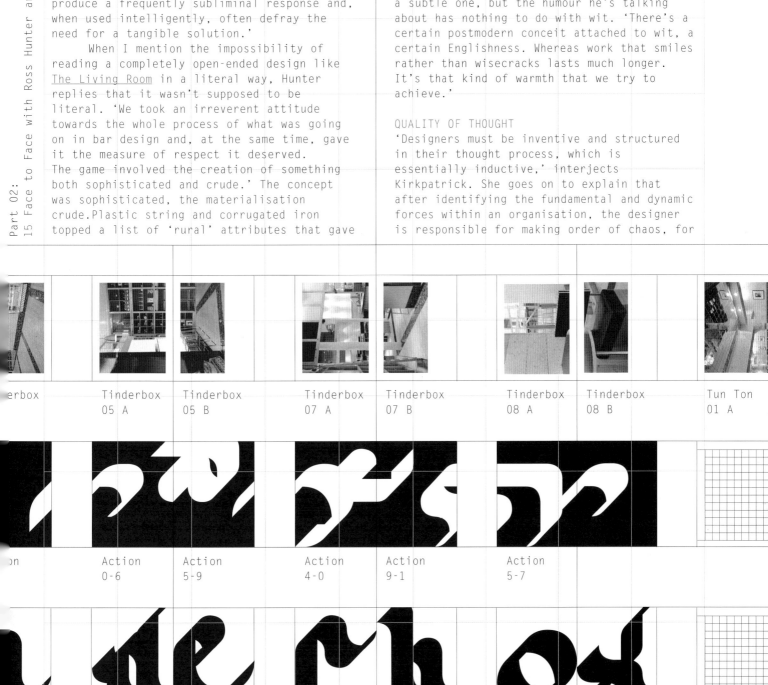

| ...erbox | Tinderbox 05 A | Tinderbox 05 B | Tinderbox 07 A | Tinderbox 07 B | Tinderbox 08 A | Tinderbox 08 B | Tun Ton 01 A |

| ...on | Action 0-6 | Action 5-9 | Action 4-0 | Action 9-1 | Action 5-7 | | |

| ...cter | Character d | Character e | Character r | Character b | Character o | Character x | |

providing the client with something that can be conveyed as a clearly articulated problem or, in the best-case scenario, as a problem resolved. 'To achieve this,' she says, 'we must be able to interpret complex and often conflicting information. It's essential to hold in-depth interviews with a client.' Without face-to-face communication, she asks, how can the designer make an accurate assessment of the organisation and its problems?

Hunter concurs. 'The starting point is always the same,' he says. 'We listen, appraise, get an understanding of the problems and objectives, and establish a brief.' The next phase is the development of a concept, which has to do with attitude and approach, with what's relevant and what's irrelevant. Development is a lengthy procedure that comprises reappraisals; testing; cost checking by means of proofs, models and samples; and market and beta testing. 'When everyone is happy,' says Hunter, 'the designer has to take the results - artwork, specifications, drawings, details, whatever - to the person who's going to make the product.' Here again, the secret ingredient is good communication. 'The process is the same whether it's for a poster, a supermarket or a helicopter,' he

adds. 'The most important aspect, however, is the quality and thoroughness of the thought that goes into it.'
Although they've used the terms 'architect' and 'designer' to describe themselves, Kirkpatrick balks at the compartmentalisation implied in such titles. 'I prefer not to label what I do,' she says. 'My reluctance is not because I'm ashamed of being called a designer, but because the word describes only part of what I do. I believe that the divisions between art, architecture and design are devised to create useful administration zones. But the different disciplines have more in common than they'd like to admit.'

Hunter and Kirkpatrick also believe that all humans are predisposed to be creative. 'Specialist education simply helps to make us more productively creative,' says the more contemplative member of the team, smiling. Concealed behind her words is a desire to communicate the message of multidimensional design for multifunctional objectives. Design born, raised and flourishing in Scotland.

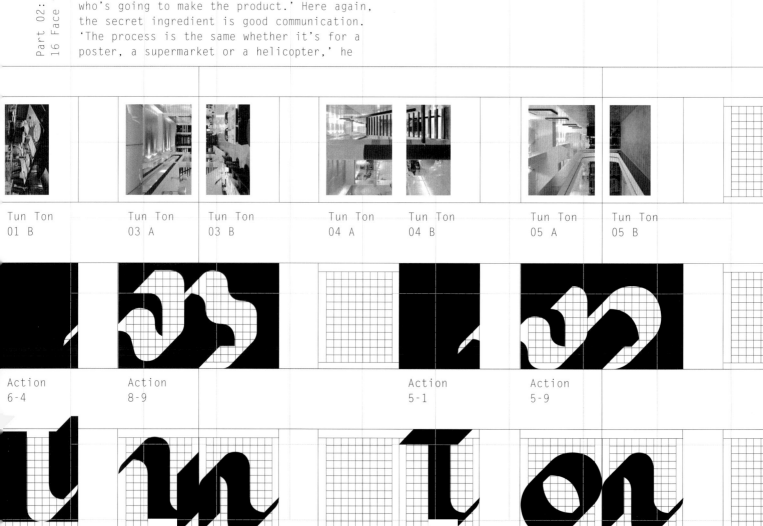

Tun Ton 01 B
Tun Ton 03 A
Tun Ton 03 B
Tun Ton 04 A
Tun Ton 04 B
Tun Ton 05 A
Tun Ton 05 B

Action 6-4
Action 8-9
Action 5-1
Action 5-9

Character T
Character u
Character n
Character T
Character o
Character n

Character a

Action
9-8

Balsa 01

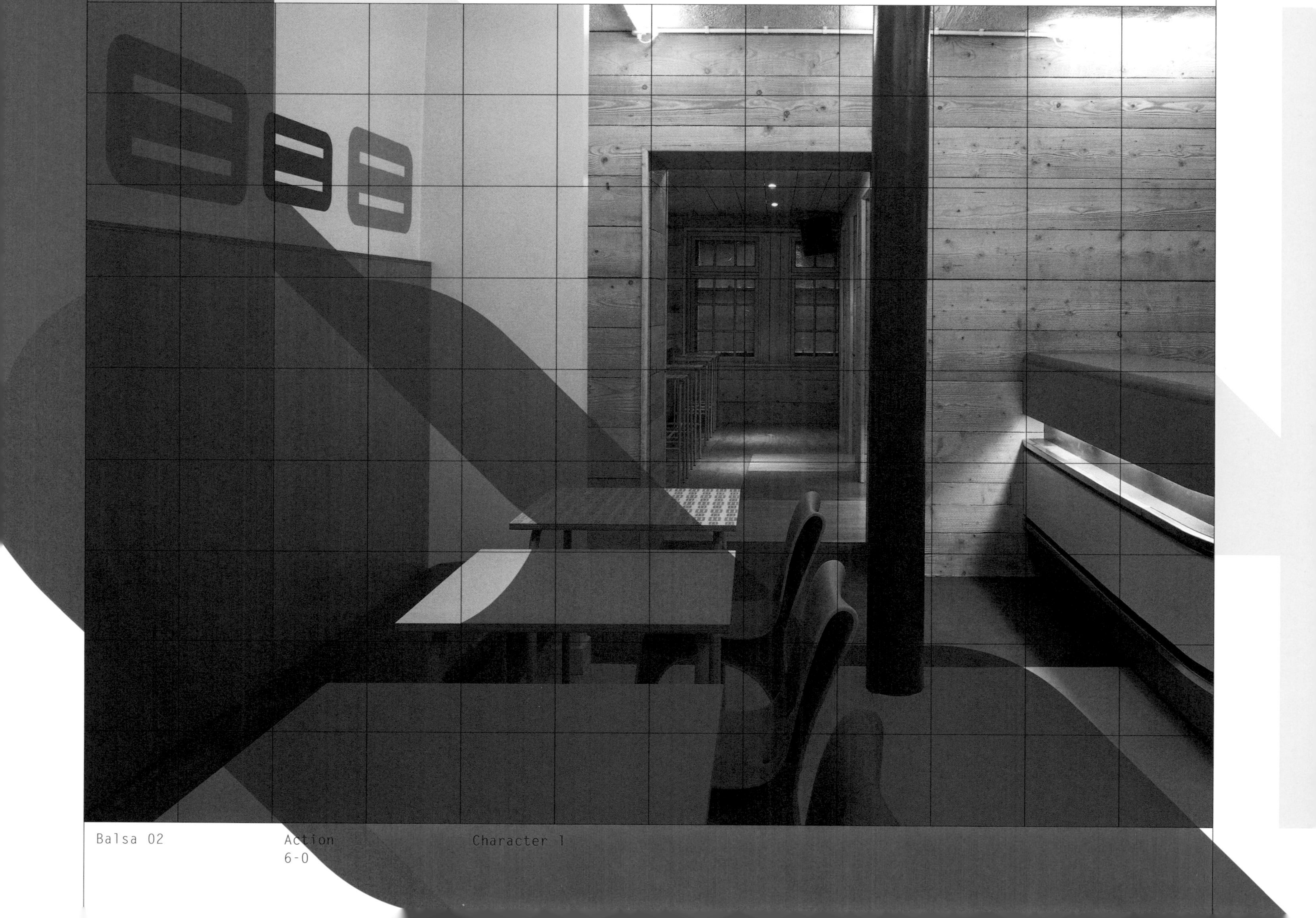

Balsa 02

Action
6-0

Character 1

Character a

Balsa 04 B

Barbazza
01 B

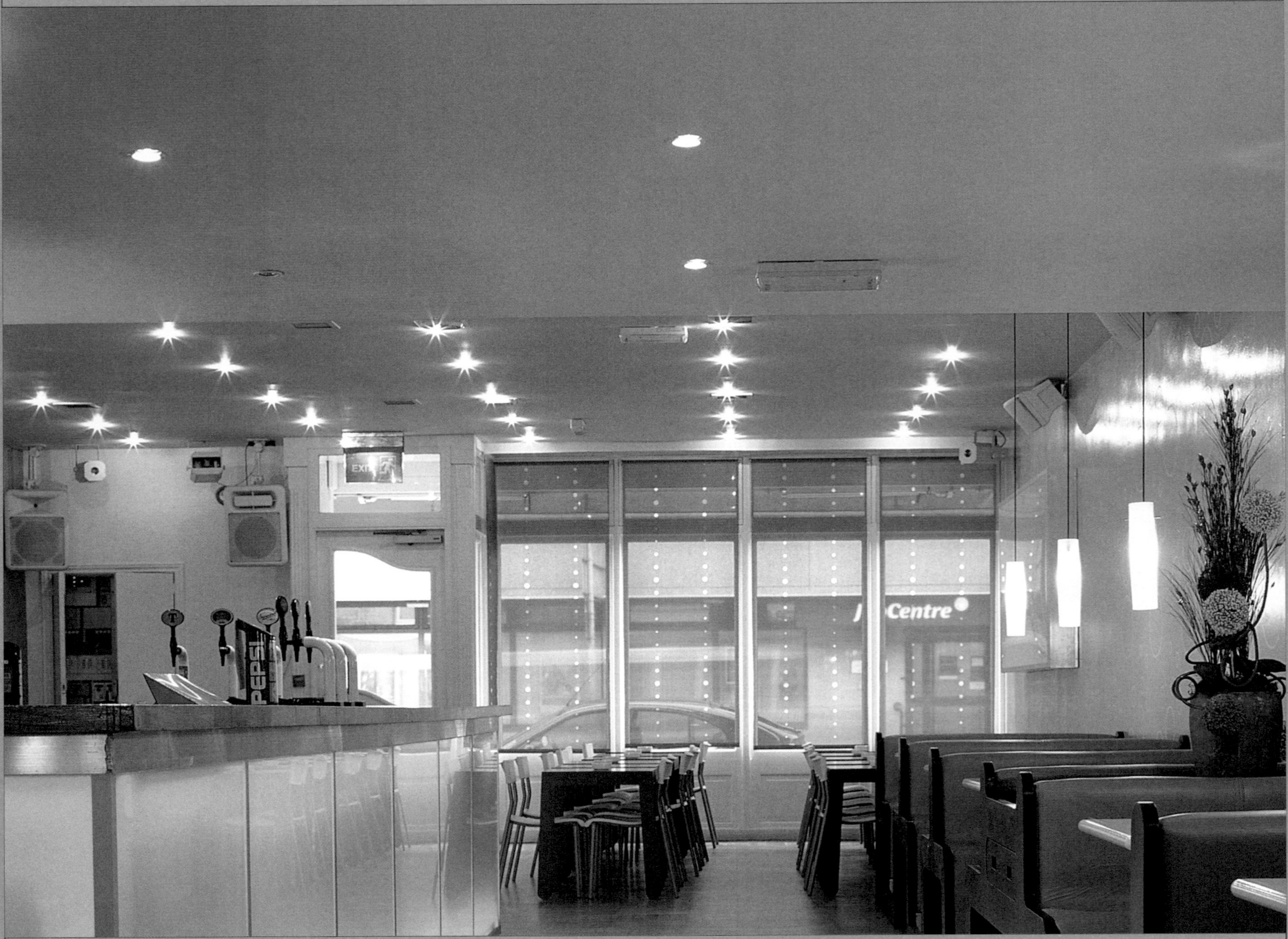

Character B

Action
5-4

Barbazza
01 B

Barbazza
02 A

Action
9-9

Character a

Part 03:
08 Barbazza

Barbazza
02 B

Action
4-0

Character

Barbazza
03 A

Action
9-4

Character

Part 03:
10 Barbazza

Barbazza
04 A

Character z

Action
6-4

Barbazza
04 B

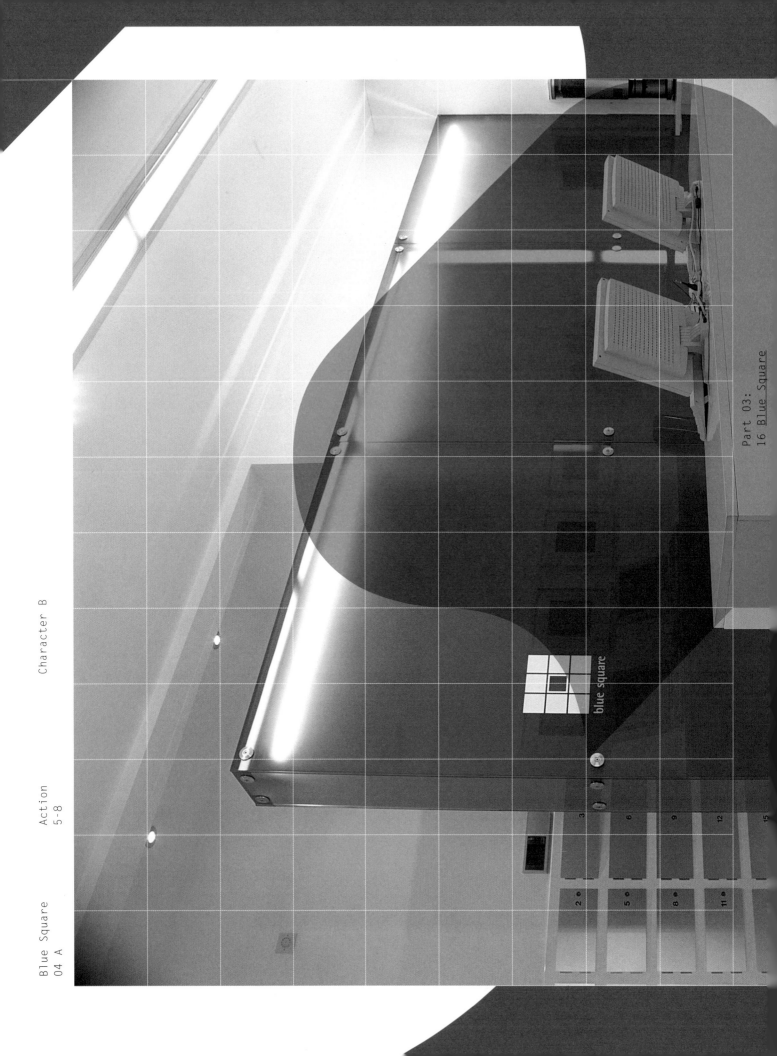

blue square

Character 1

Action-
6-7

Blue Square
04 B

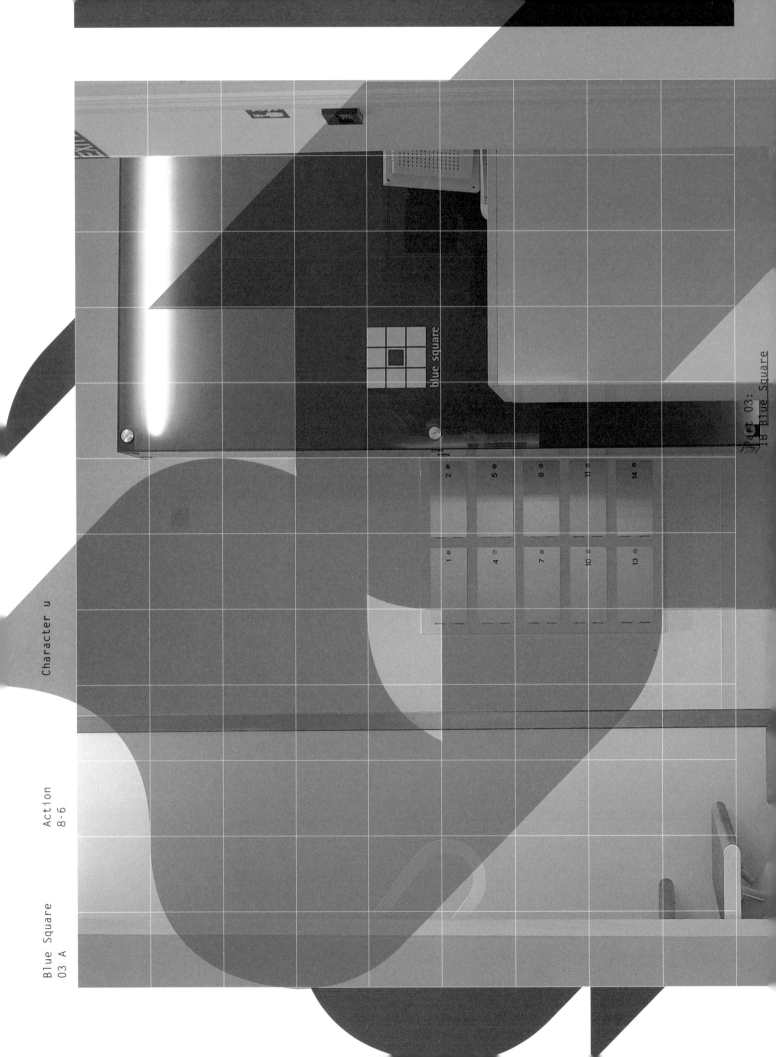

Character e

Character S

Action
5-0

Blue Square
01 B

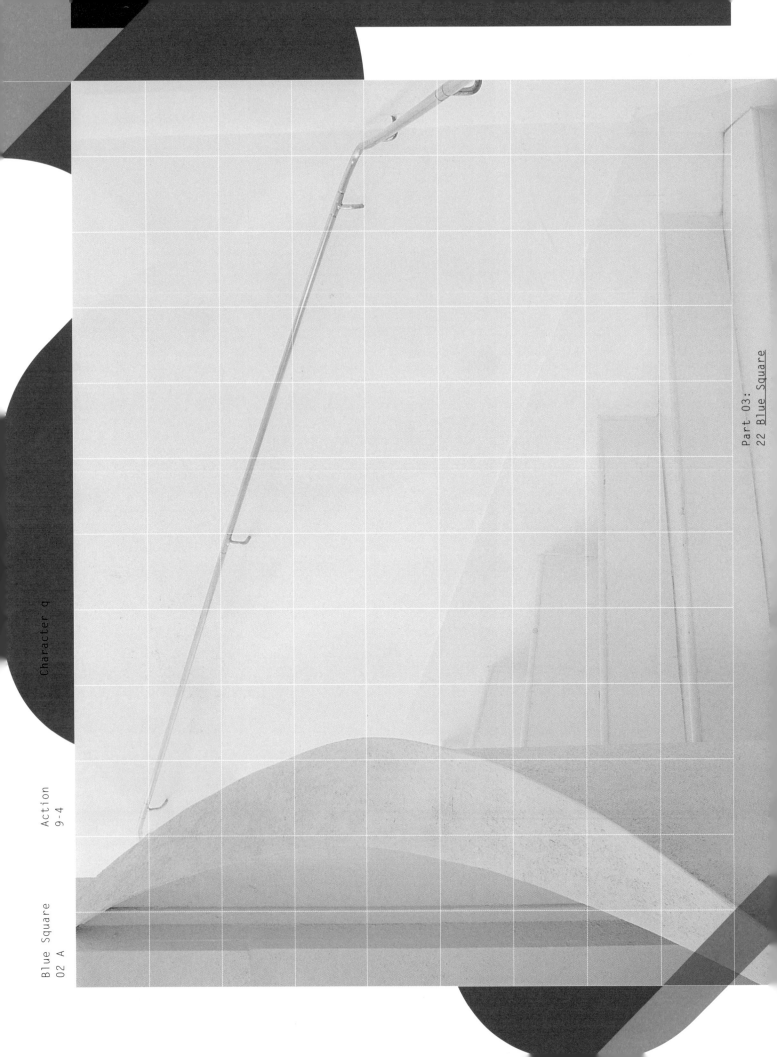

Character q

Action
9-4

Blue Square
02 A

Part 03:
23 Blue Square

Action
8-4

Character u

Blue Square
02 B

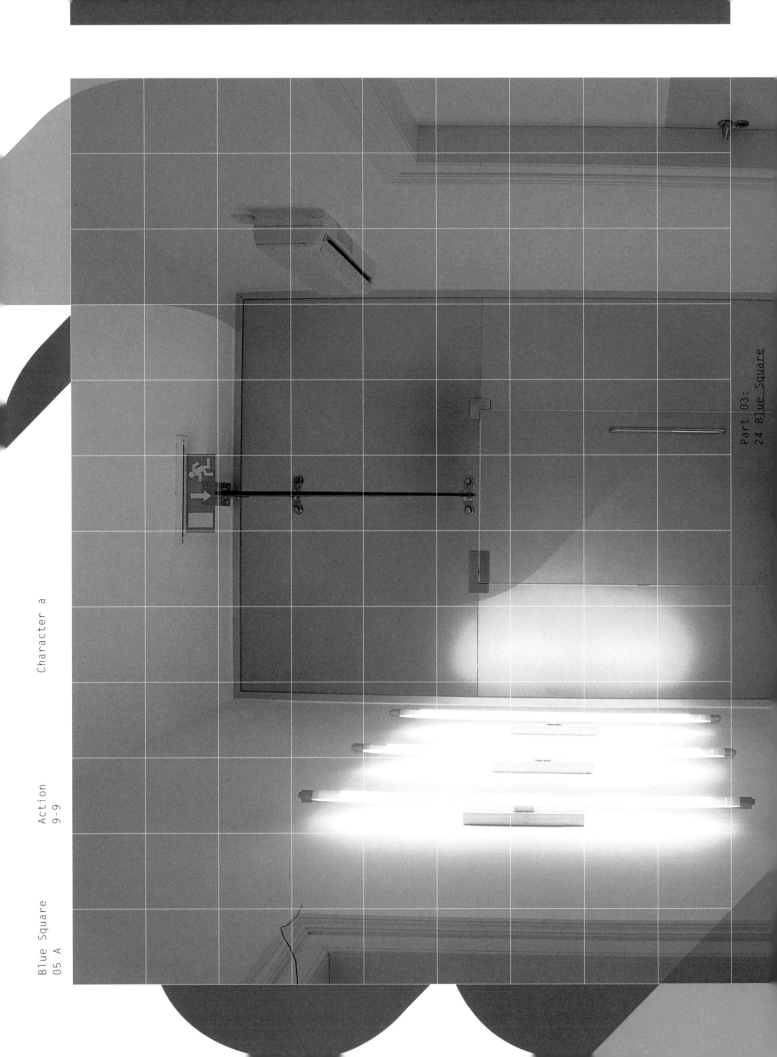

Blue Square
05 A

Action
9-9

Character a

Part 03:
24 Blue Square

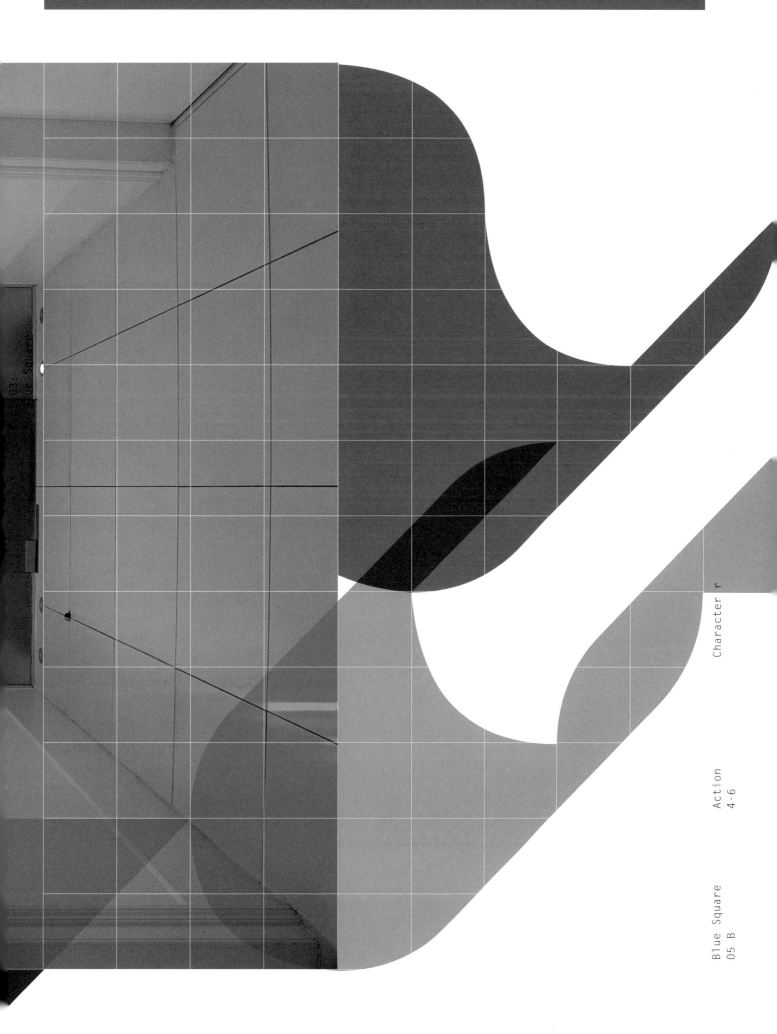

Blue Square
05 B

Action
4-6

Character r

blue square

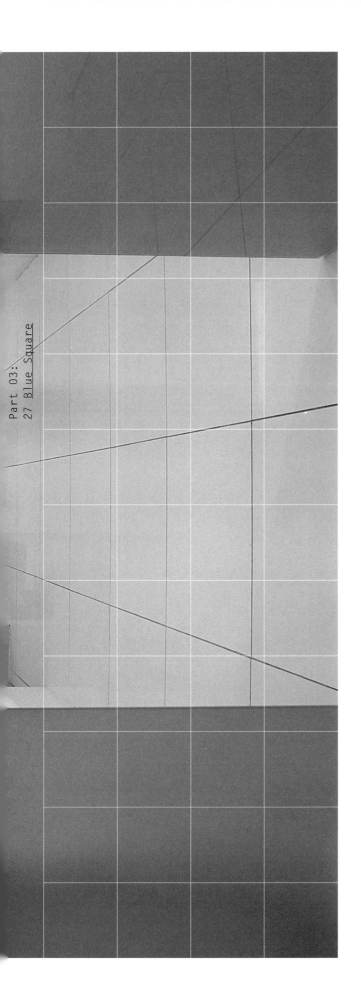

Part 03:
27 Blue Square

Action
6-0

Character T

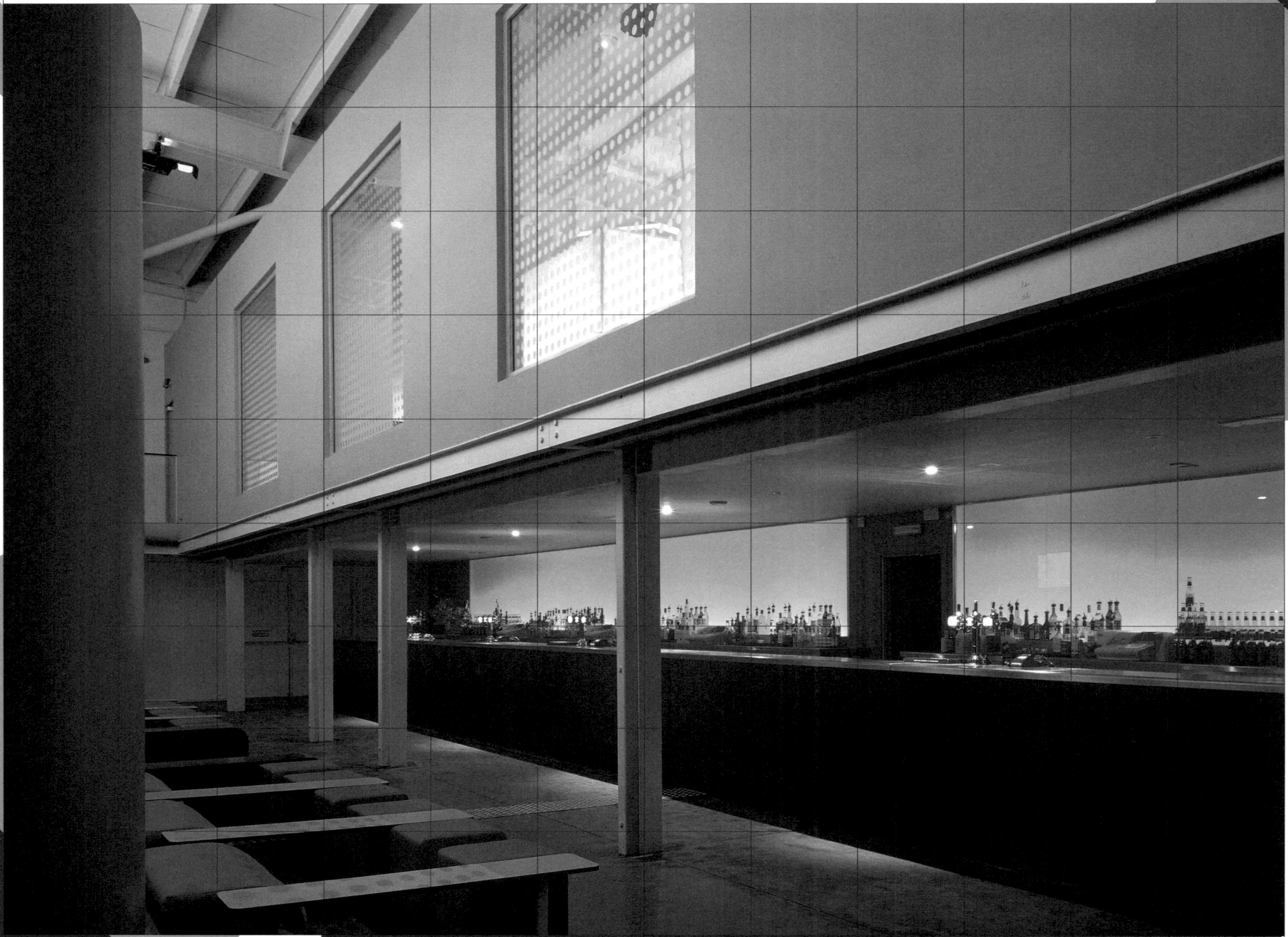

Cube 02

Action
9-6

Character h

Character e

Cube 03

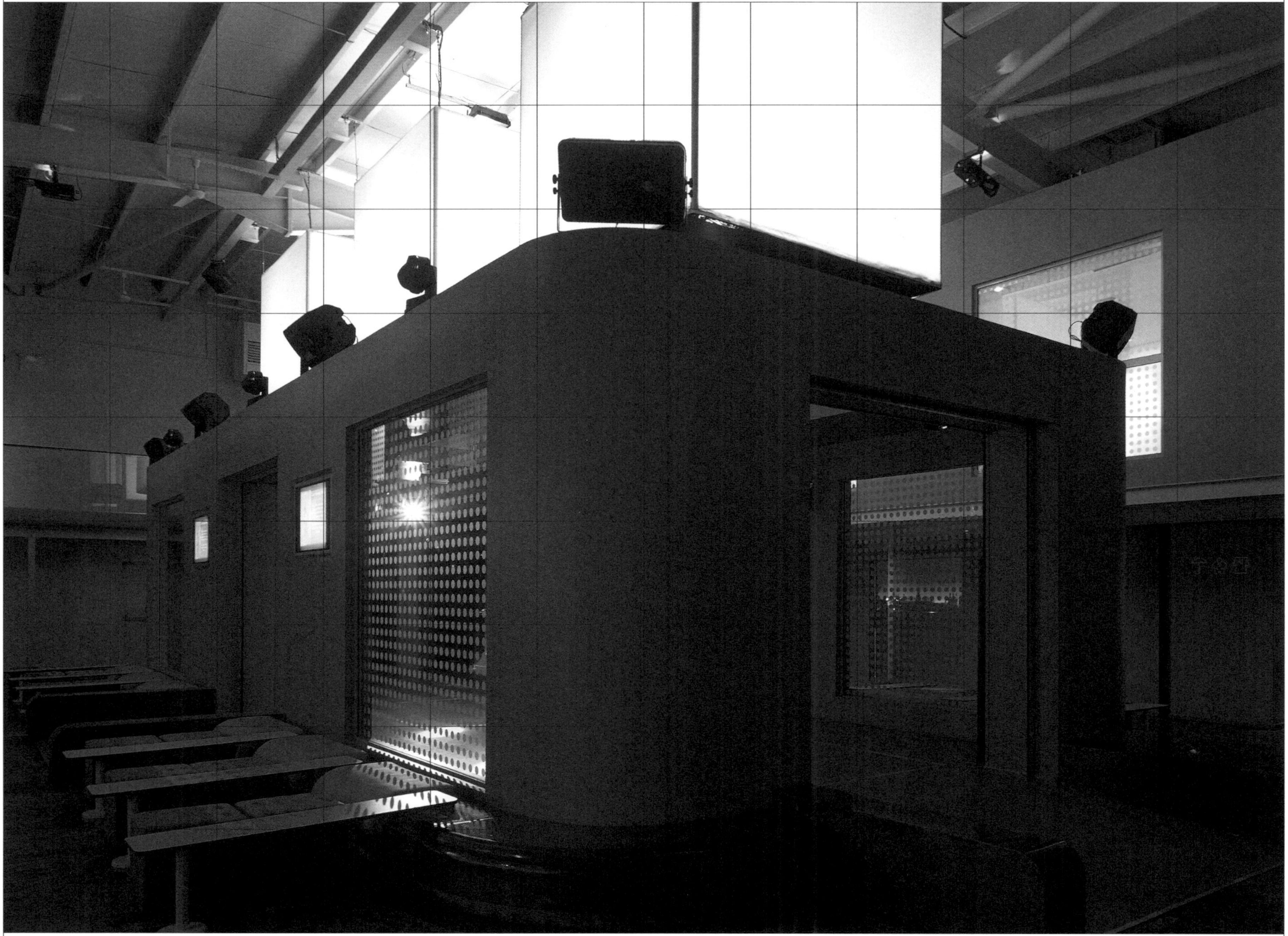

Cube 04

Cube
10 A

Action
5-4

Character C

Part 03
82 Cube

Cube 09

Action
9-6

Character b

Character e

Character i

Action
6-6

The Living Room 02   Action   Character i
6-9

Character n

Character g

The Living Room 03
A

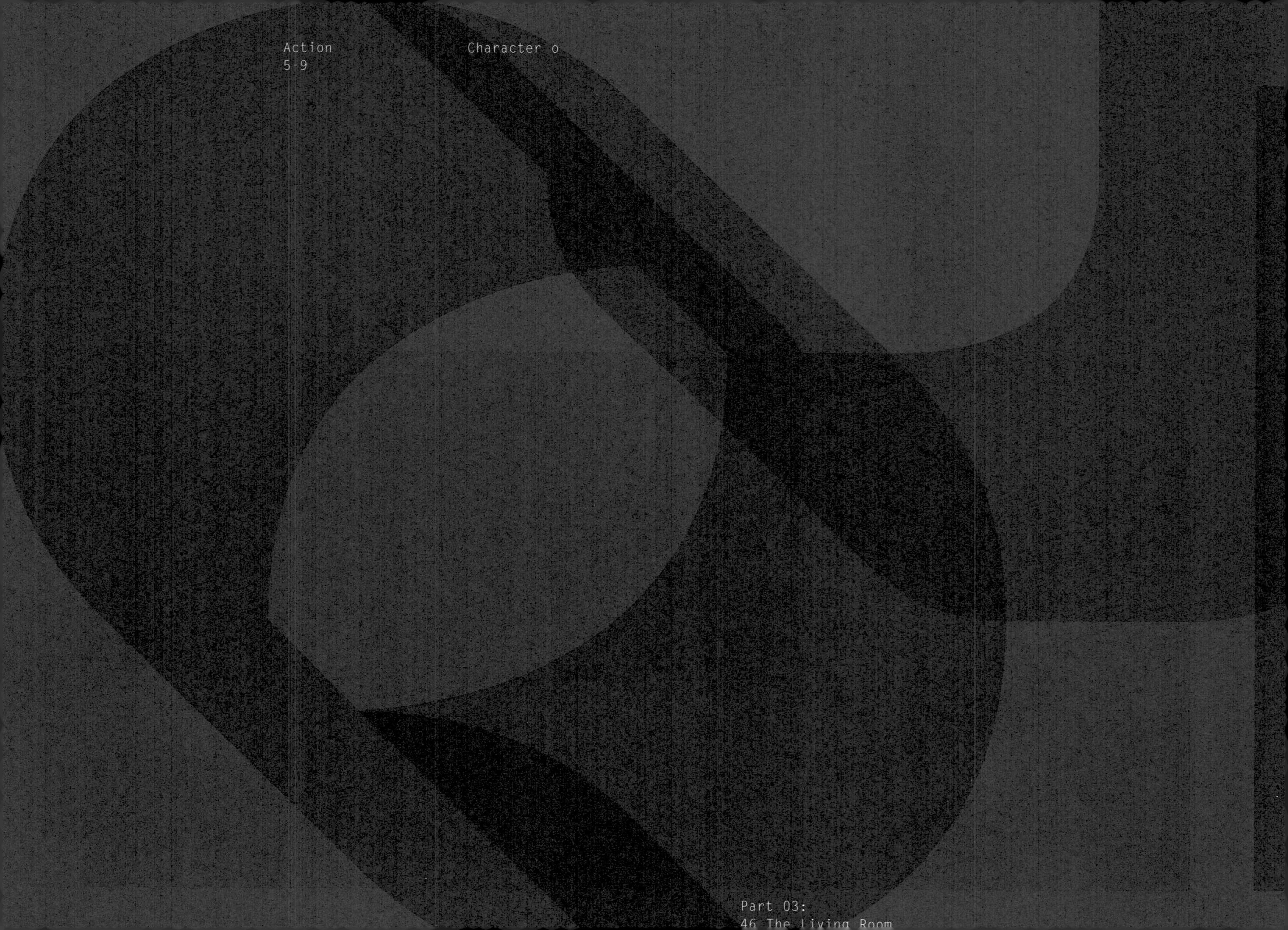
Action
5-9
Character o
Part 03:
46 The Living Room

Character m

red lemon
It's a game thing!

Character R

Red Lemon 02 B   Action
6-6

Character e

Part 03:
50 Red Lemon

Red Lemon 01 B

Character d

Red Lemon 03 A

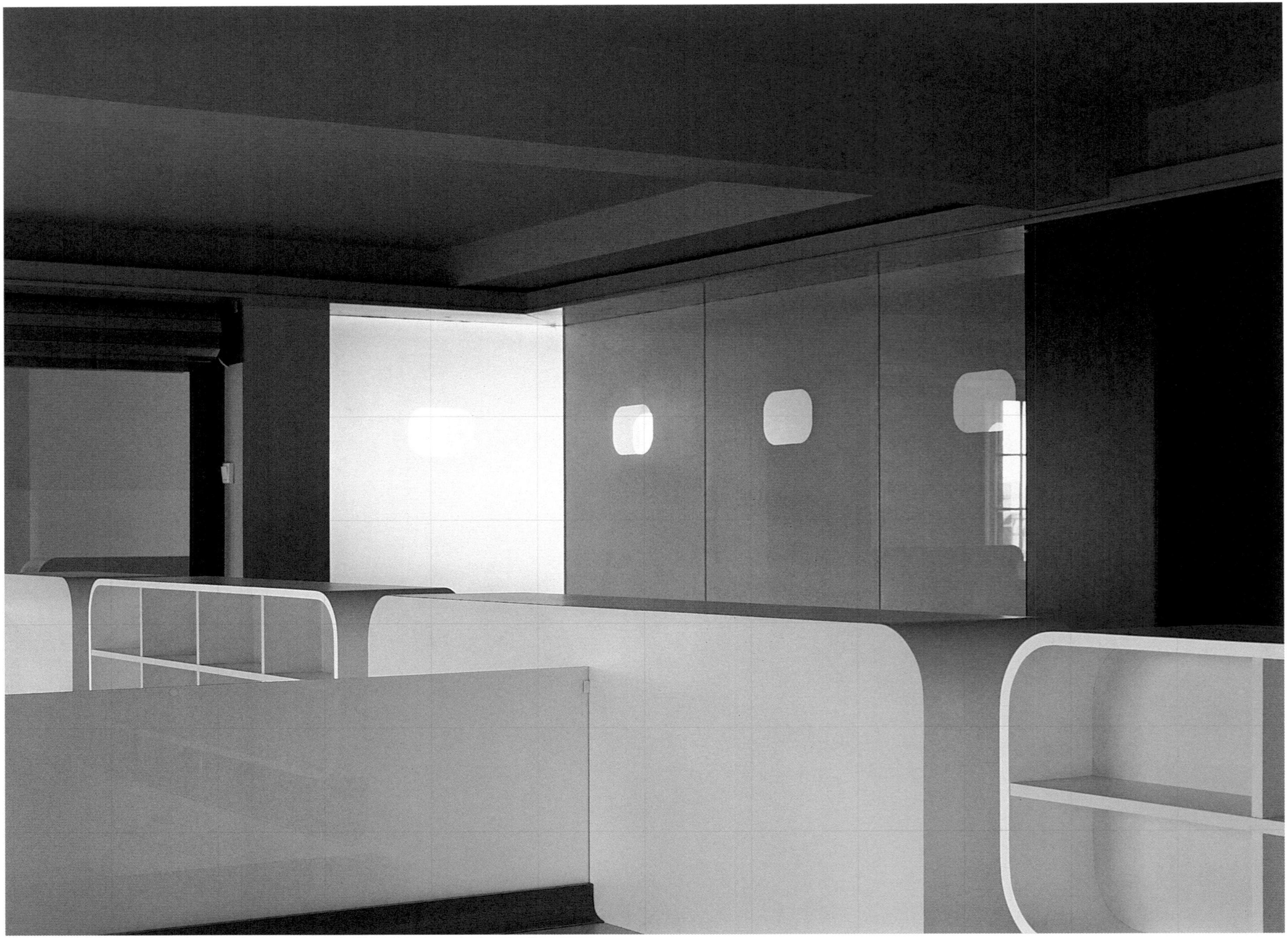

Character e

Action
5-9

Red Lemon 04

Action
7-1

Character m

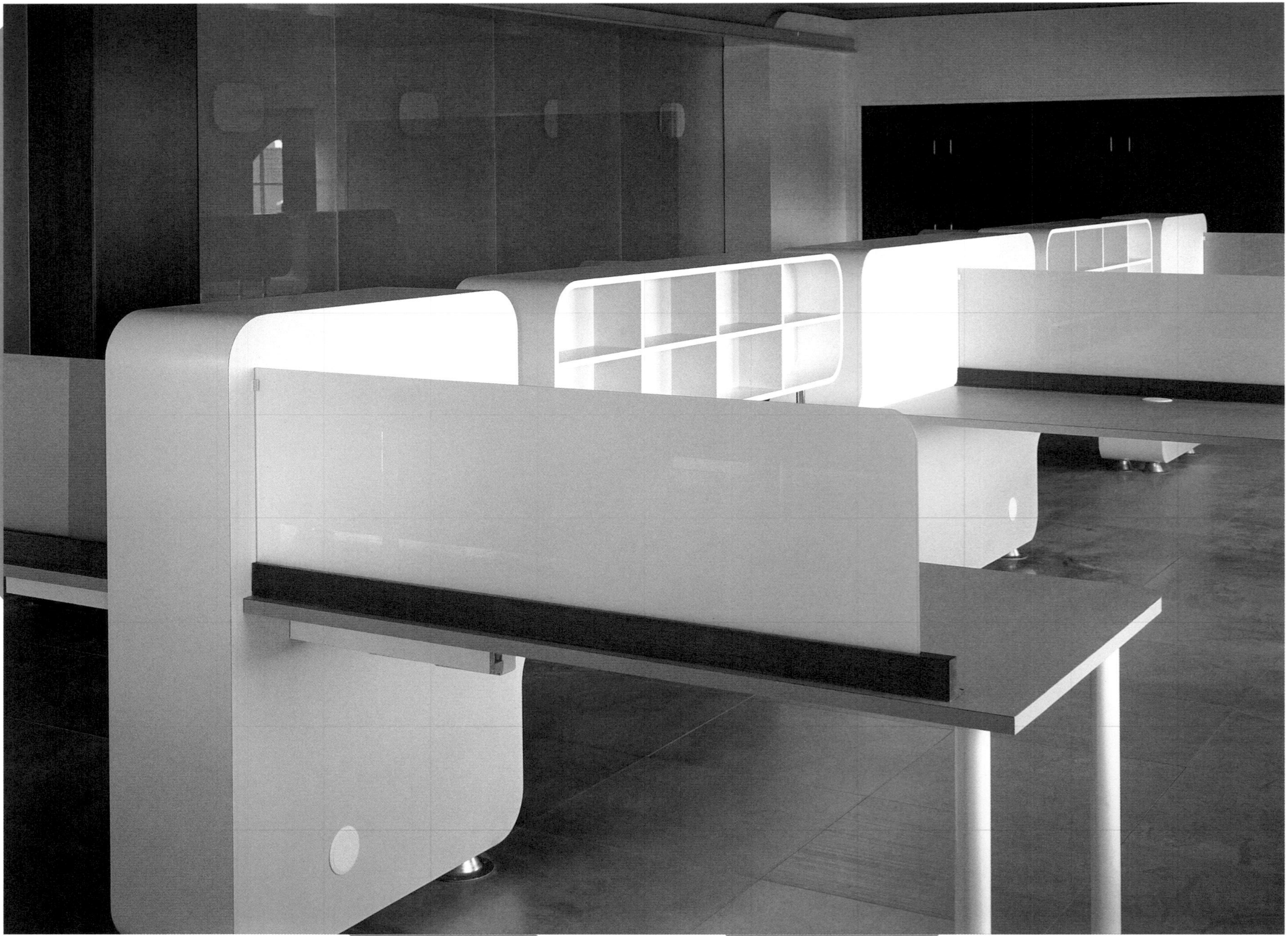

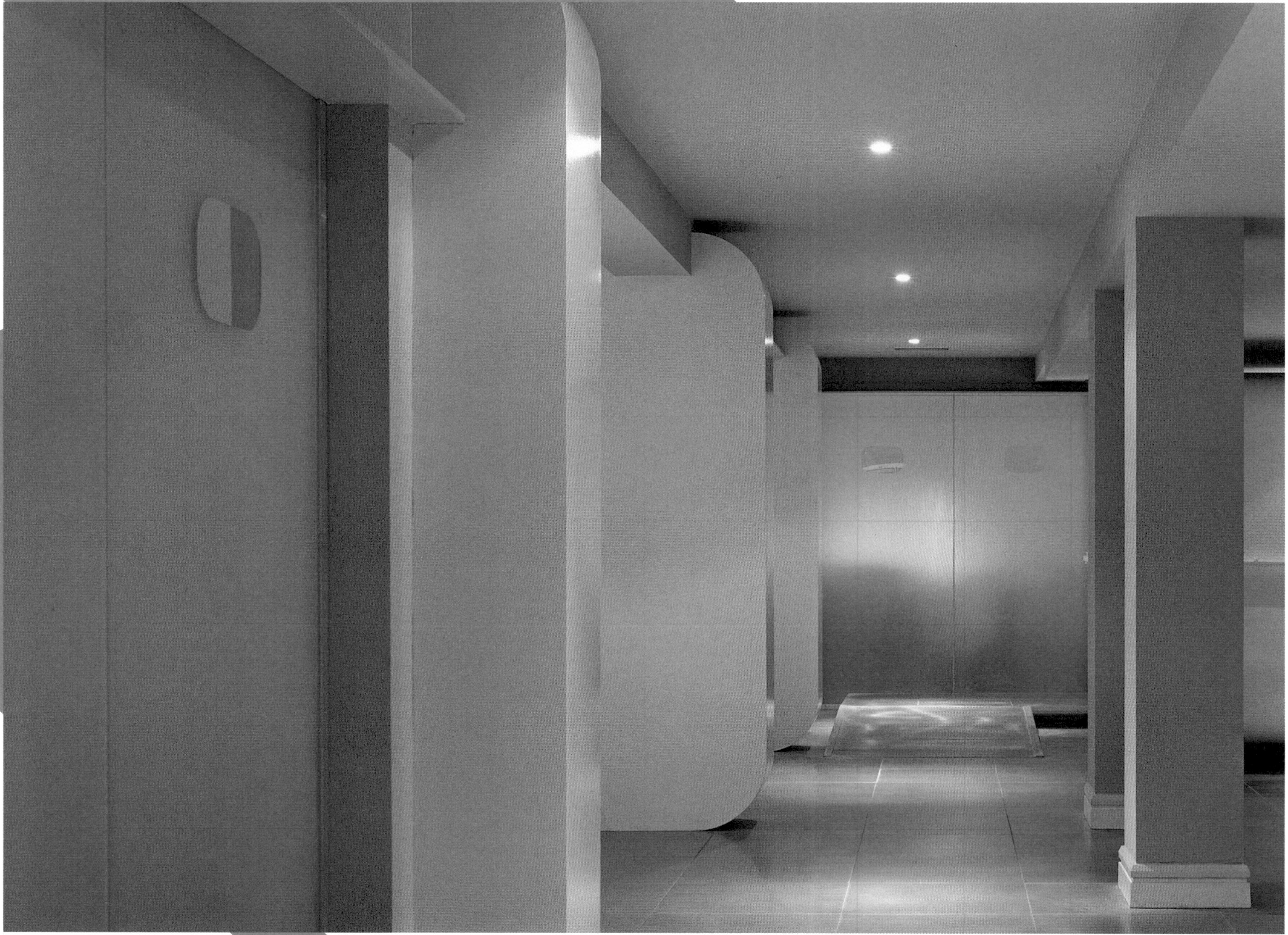

Character o

Room at the Top
04 B

Action
5-1

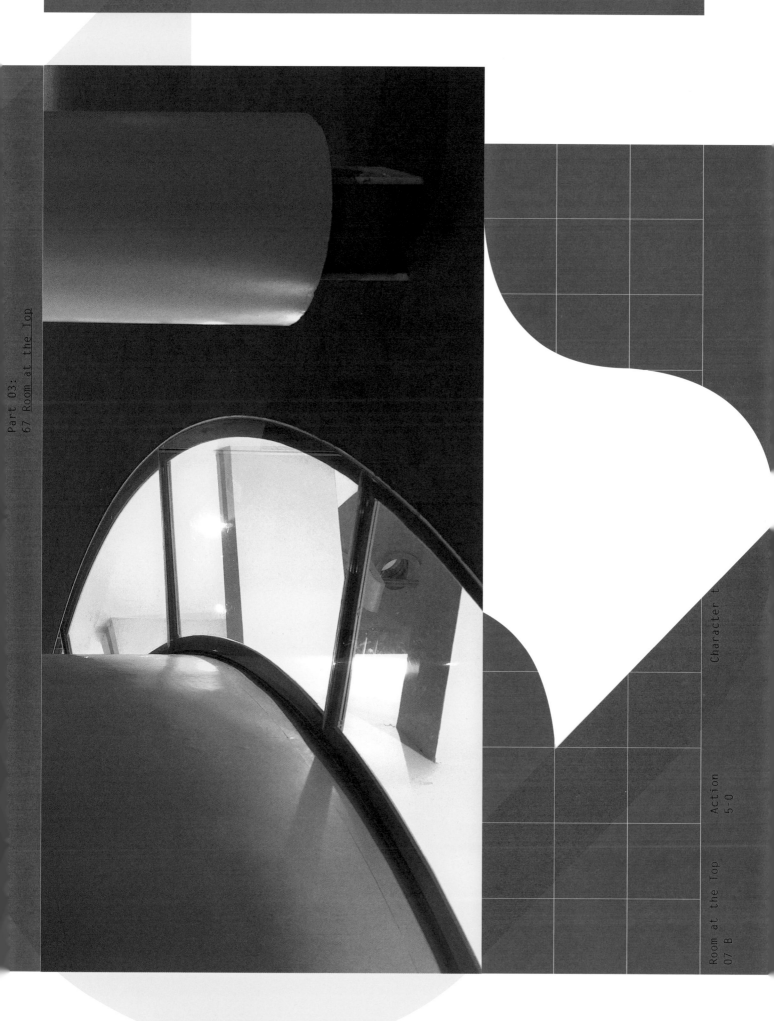

Character t

Action
5 0

Room at the Top
07 B

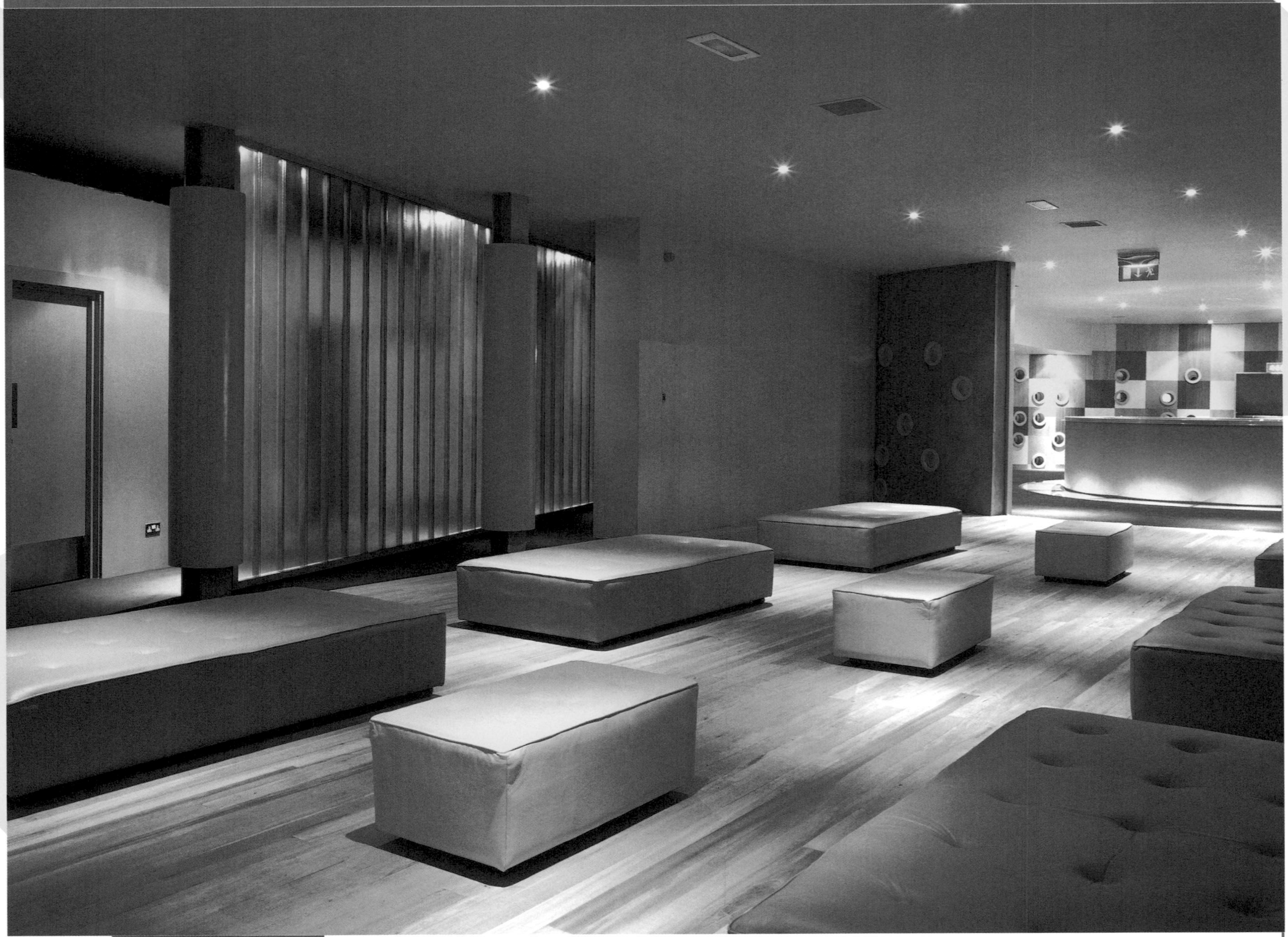

Character e

Room at the Top
06 A

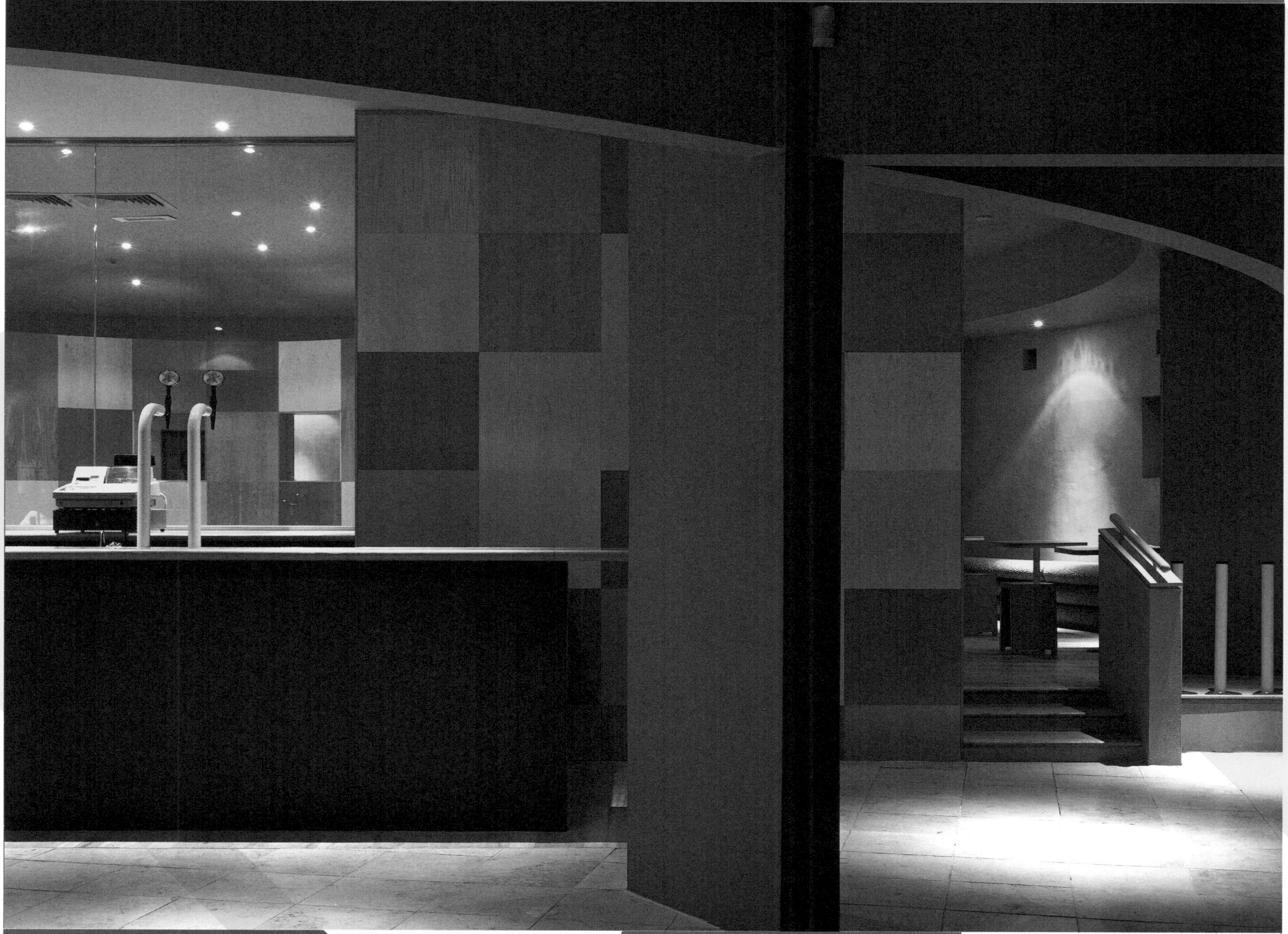

Room at the Top
03

Action
6-1

Character T

Room at the Top   Action   Character o
01   5-4

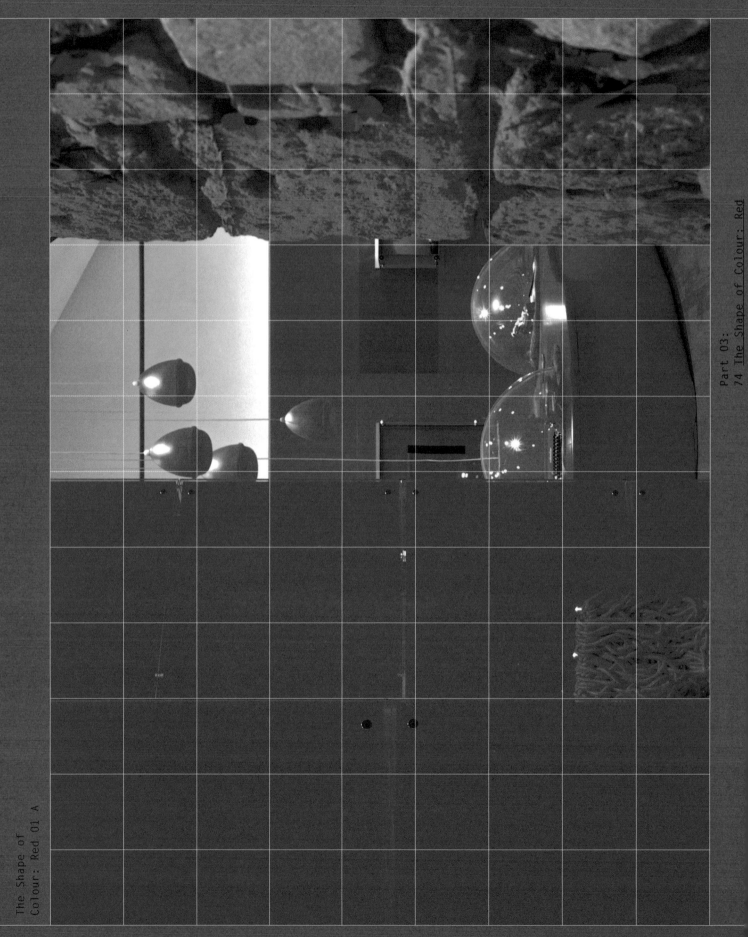

The Shape of
Colour: Red 01 A

Character e

The Shape of
Colour: Red

Action
5-7

The Shape of
Colour: Red 02

"Nature, red in tooth and claw"

Character d

The Shape of
Colour: Red 03

Character T

tion

Tinderbox

MOCHA

ORIGINAL
WHITE
SPICY
ICEBOX

OTHER COFFEE

ESTATE DRIP COFFEE

CAPPUCCINO

ORIGINAL
SKINNY

LATTE

ORIGINAL
SKINNY
VANILLA or CINNAMON
CARAMEL
VANILLA ICEBOX
CARAMEL ICEBOX

ESPRESSO

SINGLE
DOUBLE
RISTRETTO

MACCHIATO
CON PANNA
AMERICANO

Action
0-6

Tinderbox
05 A

Action
5-9

Tinderbox
05 B

Character b

Action
9-1

Tinderbox
07 B

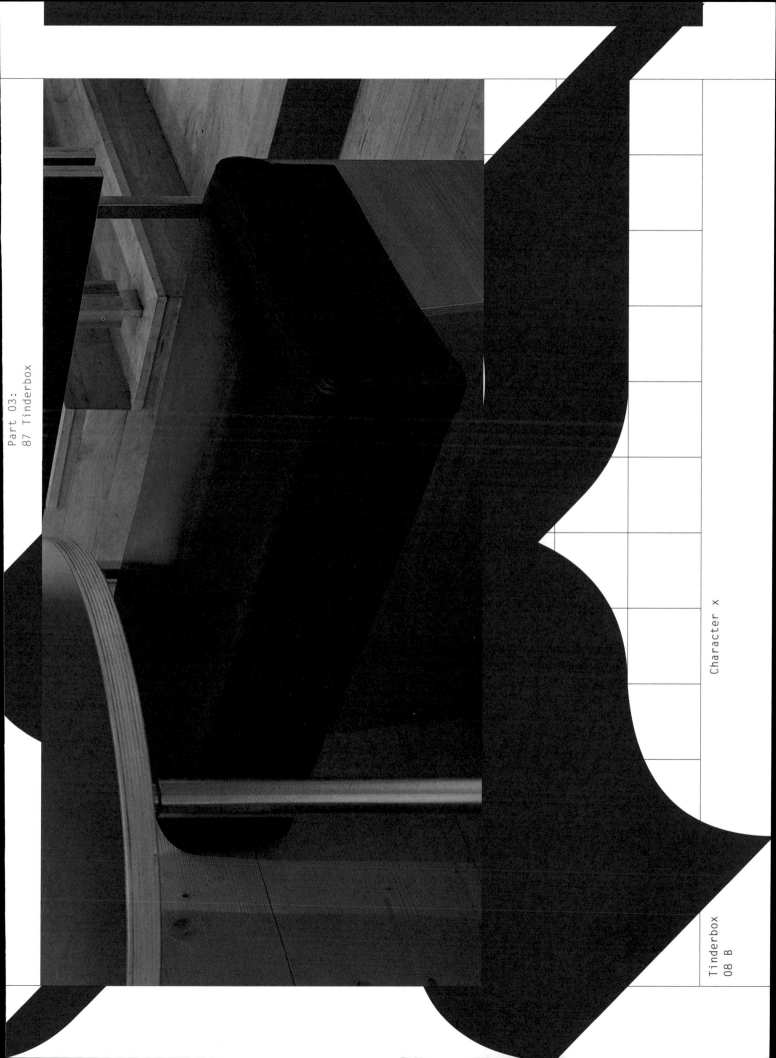

Character x

Tun Ton
01 A

Character u

Action
8-9

Tun Ton
01 A

Character n

Tun Ton
01 A

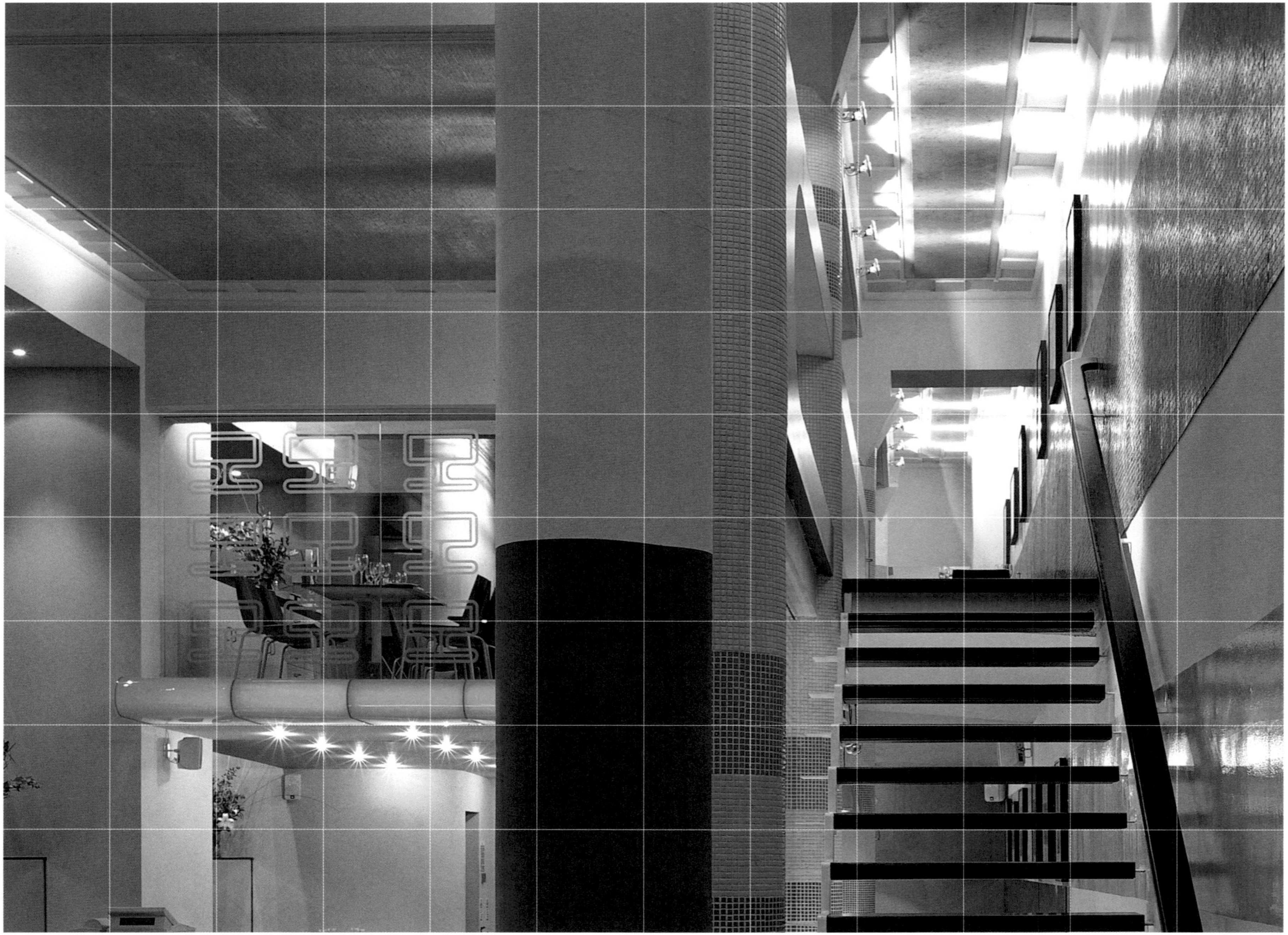

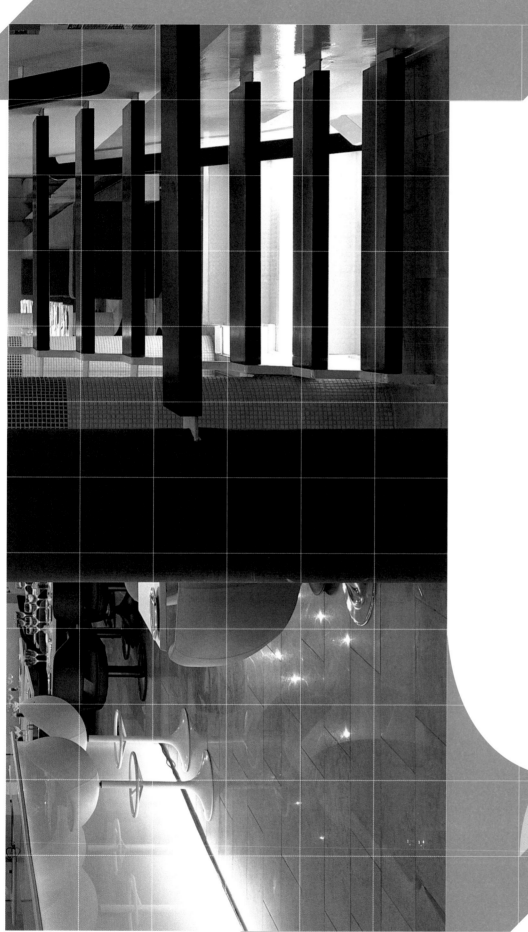

Character T

Action
5-1

Tun Ton
01 A

Character 0

Action
5-9

Tun Ton
01 A

Character n

Tun Ton
01 A

Project

Action

Character

Part 03:
96